# About This Book

## Why is this topic important?

People have always had a need to learn from people who aren't in their immediate vicinity. In the Middle Ages, for example, craft guilds provided opportunities to apprentice and learn from experts. Craft workers traveled great distances to learn from the best. Today's technologies allow us to do similar sharing but at a distance. Early models of distance learning—correspondence study, for example—were text-based because books and paper were the technology that was available at the time. As technologies change and expand, the options for learning expand with them. Because the Internet exists, it can and will be harnessed for learning. Our task is to use the technology effectively.

## What can you achieve with this book?

The book will help you

- Understand the terms, jargon, and technologies involved in online learning
- Realize how all these elements fit together
- Feel confident about taking the next step to learn more
- Become your own decision maker

For instance, before helping your organization choose the best learning management system (LMS), you have to know what an LMS is, what it does, and how to choose one. The book will provide this baseline information in a nonthreatening way that cuts through the hype.

## How is the book organized?

Each chapter begins by laying out some questions you've probably had about online learning. Most of the questions don't have strictly right or wrong answers, so we don't claim to provide only one right answer;

instead, we'll use these questions as guideposts to help you navigate through the ideas in each chapter.

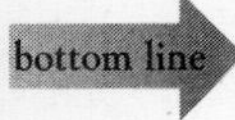


Throughout the book, you'll see an icon next to sentences in boldface type. These are "bottom line" ideas—ideas that capture or summarize the chapter's most important points.

This book provides plenty of information to give you a baseline knowledge of the tools, technologies, and issues involved in online learning, but the next step—jumping in and learning more about the areas that are most relevant to your own needs and situation—is up to you. To help you do that, each chapter ends by pointing you to the companion Web site for this book: **www.learningpeaks.com/msoll**. There you'll find additional resources to help you learn more about specific topics that interest you.

# About Pfeiffer

Pfeiffer serves the professional development and hands-on resource needs of training and human resource practitioners and gives them products to do their jobs better. We deliver proven ideas and solutions from experts in HR development and HR management, and we offer effective and customizable tools to improve workplace performance. From novice to seasoned professional, Pfeiffer is the source you can trust to make yourself and your organization more successful.

**Essential Knowledge** Pfeiffer produces insightful, practical, and comprehensive materials on topics that matter the most to training and HR professionals. Our Essential Knowledge resources translate the expertise of seasoned professionals into practical, how-to guidance on critical workplace issues and problems. These resources are supported by case studies, worksheets, and job aids and are frequently supplemented with CD-ROMs, Web sites, and other means of making the content easier to read, understand, and use.

**Essential Tools** Pfeiffer's Essential Tools resources save time and expense by offering proven, ready-to-use materials—including exercises, activities, games, instruments, and assessments—for use during a training or team-learning event. These resources are frequently offered in looseleaf or CD-ROM format to facilitate copying and customization of the material.

Pfeiffer also recognizes the remarkable power of new technologies in expanding the reach and effectiveness of training. While e-hype has often created whizbang solutions in search of a problem, we are dedicated to bringing convenience and enhancements to proven training solutions. All our e-tools comply with rigorous functionality standards. The most appropriate technology wrapped around essential content yields the perfect solution for today's on-the-go trainers and human resource professionals.

*Essential resources for training and HR professionals*

Patti Shank and Amy Sitze

# Making Sense of Online Learning

A Guide for Beginners and the Truly Skeptical

Published by Pfeiffer
An Imprint of Wiley
989 Market Street, San Francisco, CA 94103-1741 www.pfeiffer.com



For additional copies/bulk purchases of this book in the U.S. please contact 800-274-4434. Pfeiffer books and products are available through most bookstores. To contact Pfeiffer directly, call our Customer Care Department within the U.S. at 800-274-4434, outside the U.S. at 317-572-3985, fax 317-572-4002, or www.pfeiffer.com.

Pfeiffer also publishes its books in a variety of electronic formats. Some content that appears in print may not be available in electronic books.



**Library of Congress Cataloging-in-Publication Data**

Shank, Patti, 1954-
Making sense of online learning: a guide for beginners and the truly skeptical / Patti Shank and Amy Sitze.
p. cm.
Includes bibliographical references and index.
ISBN 0-7879-6982-6 (alk. paper)
1. Internet in education. 2. Computer-assisted instruction. I. Sitze, Amy, 1971- II. Title.
LB1044.87.S517 2004
371.33'44678—dc22

2003028271

Acquiring Editor: Matthew Davis
Director of Development: Kathleen Dolan Davies
Production Editor: Nina Kreiden
Editor: Suzanne Copenhagen
Manufacturing Supervisor: Bill Matherly
Editorial Assistant: Laura Reizman
Cover Design: Hatty Lee
Illustrations: Lotus Art

Printed in the United States of America
Printing 10 9 8 7 6 5 4 3 2 1

# Contents

# List of Tables and Figures

# Introduction

## *Getting the Most from This Resource*

Are you wondering about online learning? Maybe you've been given the task of developing online instructional materials but the jargon and seemingly endless technical considerations have you stopped cold. Or perhaps you're wondering if all this technology-for-learning enthusiasm is mostly hype and not worth the bytes it's written on. You're not alone—and your fears have merit. In order to get past the hype and understand how you can use technology to help people learn, you need to first understand how these technologies work, what they can do, and how to support the people using them.

It's not rocket science. Some folks have made it seem needlessly complex because they want you to depend on their wisdom. That's a scary thought in a market where vendors and consultants come and go in the blink of an eye. It's better to develop your own wisdom, so you can evaluate the options and make the best decisions for your unique situation. That's what this book is about.

### Who Should Read This Book?

This book is for you if you're

- Just starting to use the Internet to train and educate others

- Hearing terms such as SCORM, HTML, and LMS with only a vague idea of what they stand for or what they mean for online instruction
- Tired of all the vendor hype and need a dose of reality
- Tasked with using technology to teach but don't understand what it all means or how it works
- Thinking about putting instructional content online but wondering how to proceed—or whether to proceed at all
- Convinced that what you're currently doing works fine and doesn't need to be "fixed"
- Wondering why there's so much buzz about online learning, since the results don't seem to match the excitement
- Noticing that current approaches to online learning haven't lived up to their promise and wondering whether online learning is to blame or whether it's lack of understanding about how to use it
- Being asked to help with technical aspects of online learning projects but feel a need to understand the "learning" end of it as well
- Hoping to be able to explain the basics of online learning to others

This book may be for you if you are

- A corporate trainer
- An instructional designer
- A training or curriculum administrator

- A subject matter or content expert working on instructional projects
- Someone whose work supports instructional design and development: for example, an illustrator, a multimedia developer, a graphic artist, a project manager, or a curriculum developer
- A faculty member or instructor
- An information technology (IT) professional
- An adult educator
- A chief learning officer or chief knowledge officer
- A human resources manager or generalist

## Who Should Not Read This Book?

This is a book for beginners, skeptics, and folks who want to improve the way they use the Internet for teaching, training, or educating. It's also for people who need to know about this field because they support the design, development, or implementation of instruction. If you already know a lot about using technology for learning, chances are this book isn't for you.

This is not a "cookbook" that will give you precise steps for designing an online course or buying a learning management system. We do provide loads of practical tips and examples, but this isn't a how-to manual. Instead, our goal is to give you a conceptual overview of online learning topics so you'll understand the big picture and how all the pieces fit together—and, most important, you'll know what steps you need to take next. Those "next steps" will be different for each person and situation, but this book will provide you with an excellent foundation of knowledge as you go forward. (For many people, how-to books and instructional opportunities may be the next step.)

In this book, we assume that your organization has already made the decision to use online learning in one form or another—or is strongly leaning toward it—and your biggest need right now is to get up to speed. Because of this, we briefly touch on the business advantages of using online learning but do not focus heavily on it. There are excellent books and resources that walk you through a detailed process for making the business case for online learning. The premise of this book, however, is that online learning is not necessarily the right answer for every learning need or business need. It has strong advantages in certain situations, but it isn't the only way to teach and learn. **This book won't try to convince you to use online learning; instead, it will help you figure out how and when to use it effectively.**

bottom line

## Who Are the Authors?

Patti Shank is a well-known instructional technology consultant, researcher, writer, and industry analyst who has worked on numerous higher-education, corporate, nonprofit, and government technology-based instructional projects. She is listed in *Who's Who in Instructional Technology*, wrote a monthly column for *Online Learning Magazine*, and frequently presents at training and instructional technology conferences. Patti's research on new online learners won a best paper award at EDMEDIA 2002.

Amy Sitze is a journalist and magazine editor who became fascinated with online learning during her three years as editor of *Online Learning Magazine*. She liked the straightforward, no-nonsense attitude Patti brought to the award-winning "Humble Opinion" column, and encouraged Patti to turn the ideas from the column into a book. Working together, they updated and rewrote the magazine columns and added more recent information from Patti's research and presentations.

The voice in the book—the "I" in the stories, anecdotes, and opinions—is Patti's voice. Amy's ideas and words are included here, too, but whenever you hear someone talking in the first person, it's Patti.

## How Is This Book Organized?

This book helps you consider instructional technologies from the perspective of helping learners and organizations achieve their learning goals.

First, it outlines the bigger picture of online learning and introduces you to all those terms you may have heard but still don't understand. Then it describes the primary online learning technologies and how they work. Of course, this book also provides you with a framework for considering instructional goals: It analyzes the need for using technologies, explains the technologies involved in designing and developing instructional materials, and details the ones that help you deliver and deploy online learning. Finally, the book describes ways to assess the effectiveness of your online learning efforts.

One of the biggest advantages of using the Web for instruction is the ability to easily update materials that change frequently (such as new products or government regulations). Since this field changes quickly, too, Patti has developed a companion Web site for this book. **The site (http://www.learningpeaks.com/msoll/) will help you take the next step by providing further reading, examples of concepts discussed in the book, and so on.** The Web site is an example of the type of online learning resource that Patti's company, Learning Peaks, uses in its own courses and its clients' learning sites. In addition to being a resource for your own learning, it's a good example of how people can assist each other in becoming more expert in any given field.

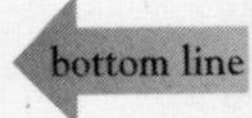


Ultimately, you can use the information in the book and Web site to help you make informed decisions about online learning for you, the learners, and your organization. After reading this book, you'll better understand how to make smart long-term decisions that work for all stakeholders.

If you're new to this field and are nervous about online learning, this book will help because it's about common sense. It will reassure you that learners and organizations can benefit from technologies when those technologies are used for the right reasons and with learning in mind.

## Frequently Asked Questions (FAQ)

In my consulting business and speaking engagements, these are some of the questions I most often hear from my clients and students about online learning:

*Why Online Learning?*

Distance learning has been around for a long time and has used various media (print, TV, satellite, networks) to support communication and learning. There has been and will always be a need to reach people who can't easily be reached through traditional face-to-face methods. Changes in society and the increasing need to train and retrain people mean the need to teach and learn at a distance will escalate. Some of the main benefits of online learning (a form of distance learning) are flexibility (people can learn at any time of day or night without being tied to a class schedule), consistency (everyone gets the same quality of training, regardless of where they're located), and quick dissemination of critical knowledge.

*Want more? See Chapter 1.*

*All of My Competitors Are Doing Online Learning. Do I Need to Do It, Too, Just to Keep Up?*

Of course not! Online learning works well in some circumstances and for some organizations and not so well in others. You need to do a thorough analysis to see whether it makes sense for your organization and learners. It makes the most sense if the learners want or need it, have easy access to it (and time to use it), and designers or developers have the resources to build and maintain it.

*Want more? See Chapter 1.*

### *What Skills Do I Need to Develop Online Instructional Materials?*

One of the reasons this field is intimidating to instructors, faculty, trainers, and teachers is that it demands a wide variety of skills. The good news is that you don't need to be an expert in every single one of those skills. Most of us work in teams with graphic designers, programmers, multimedia developers, and technical writers. If you're in a situation where you have to do most of the work yourself, it's possible to become proficient in a number of the skill areas, but give yourself some time. My advice? Start with instructional design skills for online learning and then use a standard Web authoring tool such as Dreamweaver to author simple materials.

*Want more? Read the whole book, but start with Chapter 1.*

### *Is Technology-Based Learning Better than Classroom-Based Learning?*

There aren't any hard and fast rules about this. There's good and bad classroom-based instruction and good and bad technology-based instruction. Classroom learning isn't the gold standard—it's simply what we're used to. A better question is which instructional methods work best in which circumstances, and which technologies best support them. Good instruction is less about media and more about methods. And it's not an either-or situation. Often, a combination of classroom and distance learning works best.

*Want more? See Chapter 2.*

### *What Is Interaction and Why Is It Important to Learning?*

The purpose of instructional interaction is to allow learners to apply their skills in real life, not just read or think about what they've learned. Good interactive activities create a feedback loop that influences the activity and the learner. Unfortunately, much of the online learning that's currently out there requires little from the learner and results in little learning or transfer to the real world. When we think of interaction, we often think of activities that allow the learner to interact with instructional content (animations, simulations, quizzes), but we too often leave out critical interactions with other people (discussions, debates, collaborative activities). Simply put, good online instruction includes interactions that truly help people learn.

*Want more? See Chapter 2.*

*Why Do People in This Field Use So Much Jargon? Will I Ever Be Able to Understand It?*

In every field, practitioners create a language that they alone understand fully. (Have you ever heard engineers talk?) Learning the language is part of entering into the practitioners' community. This field encompasses many others (instructional design, programming, multimedia, information architecture, human-computer interface studies, graphic arts, and server administration, to name a few) so the jargon tends to encompass all of them. The more you learn about this field, the less mystifying the jargon will seem to you.

*Want more? See Chapter 3.*

*Do Traditional Instructional Design Methods Work on the Web?*

Traditional instructional design provides a good starting point for learning about building instructional materials for the Web. However, instructional design for online instruction has more considerations than traditional instructional design, because more tasks and skills are involved. Instructional design for the Web also lends itself to rapid prototyping, allowing you to design and develop at the same time and make immediate changes as you get feedback. To design good instruction in any medium, of course, the most important consideration is how people learn.

*Want more? See Chapter 4.*

*How Can I Make Sure My Online Materials Are Logically Organized and Easy for the Learner to Use?*

This question is critical to the success of your instruction. There are lots of books and articles devoted to general Web usability—this book contains information about how it applies to instructional sites. The main concepts involve organizing a site so learners can find what they're looking for, supplying navigational elements that tell learners where they are and where they can go, and designing pages and content that are clear, concise, and easy to digest.

*Want more? See Chapter 4.*

*What Authoring Tools Should I Use to Build Online Learning?*

There is no one right authoring tool. (Sorry, I know that's not the answer newcomers to this field want to hear.) Most instructional developers use a combination of five or more tools. Many of us start with a tool that generates good general Web sites, such as Dreamweaver, and then add on tools that do graphics (such as Fireworks or PhotoShop), animations (such as Flash), and software simulations (such as RoboDemo). After that, you'll probably want to learn (or work with others) to build in programming and database functionality. Some folks like to use authoring tools built specifically for instruction, but many of those tools have limited functionality.

*Want more? See Chapter 5.*

*Do I Need to Know JavaScript and Other Programming Languages?*

No, you don't have to be able to program, but chances are that you'll want to use programming in your instructional materials. Authoring tools such as Dreamweaver automatically generate JavaScript code as you use the tool. At some point, you may decide that it's not too hard to learn a bit and start writing some simple code yourself.

*Want more? See Chapter 5.*

*What's the Difference Between an LMS and an LCMS?*

A learning management system (LMS) tracks and manages learners—course registrations, amount of time people spend in courses, test scores, number of attempts at taking tests, and so on. A learning content management system (LCMS) stores, catalogs, and manages content. It brings content into a central repository, catalogs it, and delivers it to learners. These technologies are often used together to provide an infrastructure for online and classroom-based learning.

*Want more? See Chapter 6.*

*What's a Learning Object and Why Is It Important?*

Learning objects are chunks of instructional content that are specially designed so they can be used simultaneously in different places. For example, graphics or animations designed as learning objects can be called up and used in more than one course. You can bring together different learning objects to build courses that meet specific learner needs. This kind of development is difficult to do and experts are still debating how to do it.

*Want more? See Chapter 6.*

*How Do I Evaluate Online Learning?*

That depends on whether you want to evaluate the learner's knowledge and skills or the course itself. Each requires different tactics. To evaluate the learner, you need to build in performance opportunities. What do you want learners to be able to do after they finish the course? Can they do it? To evaluate the course, establish goals (for instance, reduced help desk calls, cost savings, client ratings) up front and then measure how well the course meets those goals.

*Want more? See Chapter 7.*

*How Do I Stop Feeling Overwhelmed About Learning All This?*

I'll let you in on a secret: Even those of us who have been doing this a long time are sometimes overwhelmed by how much there is to learn. If you're overwhelmed, you've just taken the first step to becoming one of us. Welcome. Now take a deep breath. Take a few small steps, learn something new, and then take a few more steps. You'll get there.

*To learners everywhere.*
*Learning can be hard. Not learning is even harder.*

# 1

# Taking the Leap

When you go shopping to buy furniture for a room in your house, you don't randomly bring home individual chairs and tables you happen to like. It's more likely that you start by considering the big picture: your other furniture, the size and shape of the room, what'll be happening in that room, and your budget.

Online learning is no different. It's important to begin by understanding the overall concepts so the specific pieces will make more sense later. In this chapter, we'll answer the following big-picture questions:

- What is online learning?
- Where has online learning come from and where is it going?
- When does using technology for learning make sense?
- How can I tell whether my organization is ready?
- What is good online learning?
- What skills do I need?
- How do I stay sane?

## What Is Online Learning?

First, let's define online learning. Online learning involves the use of network technologies (such as the Internet and business networks) for delivering, supporting, and assessing formal and informal instruction.

Where and how does this happen? Via online resources and materials, electronic libraries, learning materials and courses, real-time and non-real-time discussions, chats, e-mail, conferencing, and knowledge sharing applications. It's important to note that online learning does not have to happen exclusively online. The use of technology for learning is often an adjunct to classroom and other face-to-face learning opportunities. In fact, the perception that online learning should be ALL online causes some short-sighted thinking and is one of the biggest myths about this field.

Some of the main reasons to use online learning include

- *Improved access and flexibility*. People can log in at any computer terminal, at home or at work, at any time of day or night, to complete a lesson or refer to learning materials.
- *Faster delivery and cost savings*. For organizations that need to convey targeted information that quickly becomes outdated (for example, the newest version of a product), online modules are almost always faster and cheaper than flying trainers across the country and requiring learners to sit in a classroom for a set number of hours.
- *Improved control and standardization*. In today's international business climate, many organizations have locations across the globe. Differences in individual trainers' knowledge and skills may mean learners in New Delhi are getting a different quality of training

than those in New York. Online learning presents a common, consistent message to large groups of learners regardless of location.

- *Enhanced communication and collaboration*. Certain software tools allow learners to communicate with each other, collaborate on projects, and share documents without the need for travel.

Whether or not you're keen on using technology for learning, the fact is that it's here to stay. Technology has become an essential way to handle the education, training, and retraining needs of an expanding knowledge society. According to a recent report on job skills, 50 percent of all employee skills become outdated in three to five years. In addition, experts say the percentage of jobs that fit into the category of "knowledge workers" is rapidly increasing (Moe & Blodgett, 2000). Even jobs that were traditionally thought to require fewer skills, such as retail sales, now commonly require computer skills and the ability to keep pace with product changes. Many blue-collar workers regularly use computers and databases in their work. We simply don't have the capacity to support today's educational needs by using traditional methods alone.

## Where Has Online Learning Come from and Where Is It Going?

The idea of using computers to help people learn has been around since the advent of computers, but it wasn't until the first Web browser was marketed in 1994 that true "online" learning—in other words, learning done through a network such as the Internet or an intranet—started to take its current shape. Corporations, government entities, nonprofits, and universities began to realize the advantages of training large numbers of geographically dispersed people via the Internet, and vendors emerged to provide them with the products and services they needed to make the idea a reality.

Some companies were early adopters, throwing themselves wholeheartedly into online learning and making it a top organizational priority. The buzz began to build, and as the dot-com frenzy grew, so did optimism about online learning. At Comdex in 1999, Cisco CEO John Chambers made his oft-quoted statement: "The next big killer application for the Internet is going to be education. Education over the Internet is going to be so big it is going to make e-mail usage look like a rounding error."

Building on Chambers' enthusiasm, research organizations such as GartnerGroup (in Stamford, Connecticut) and International Data Corp. (IDC, in Framingham, Massachusetts) began publishing figures that forecast a mind-boggling growth in e-learning. In 2001, IDC figures predicted the U.S. e-learning industry would reach $14.7 billion by 2004 (Anderson and Brennan, 2001).

A quick scan of the U.S. e-learning marketplace in late 2003 showed that e-learning didn't get anywhere close to even the lowest figures from a few years ago. According to IDC, the industry had reached only $3.6 billion at the end of 2002 (Brennan, 2003). So much for making e-mail look like a rounding error.

The good news, though, is that in companies across the world, learning professionals have continued to refine the ways they develop, design, and implement online learning. In an October 2001 survey conducted by *Online Learning Magazine* and IDC, 82 percent of respondents said they were satisfied or very satisfied with their organizations' e-learning initiatives (Kiser, 2001).

Though the intense hype that once swirled around this industry has mellowed, there's still a major place for online learning. That means you'll need to know what's what. Some of the jargon continues to confuse those of us in the training and learning business. You've probably heard your colleagues and competitors use phrases such as "end-to-end business-to-business solution" and "human capital management." Figuring out what these terms and acronyms really mean only seems to get more difficult, especially when there are several words that mean the same thing. Trust me, even those of us who make our living in this field have found ourselves perplexed by the seemingly endless jargon.

So let's tackle some of the basics and get you off to a good start.

## When Does Using Technology for Learning Make Sense?

Since technology is part of the future landscape of learning, knowing when to use it (and when not to) is the first step toward making sense of online learning.

In a nutshell, online learning makes the most sense when it directly meets the needs of learners and organizations. For instance, if an organization needs to provide ongoing instructional opportunities for dispersed learners and has the right resources and support, technology can be very helpful. On the learner side, technology can be a big plus for learners who have specific learning goals, have adequate support, and are willing and able to accept learning at a distance.

In fact, technology can provide access to people, opportunities, mentoring, help, and information that wouldn't be available otherwise. Used well, it can be a powerful tool. Used poorly or thoughtlessly, however, technology can get in the way of organizational and individual needs. Clients sometimes tell me that their CEO wants to use online learning because "it's faster, cheaper, and better." **Be skeptical about generic claims about what technology will do. When technology is used improperly, for the wrong reasons, or without the proper resources in place, it's likely to be slow, expensive, and inefficient.**

bottom line

Use Table 1.1 as a starting place to help you organize your thoughts about when online learning makes sense.

Table 1.1. When Does Online Learning Make Sense? When Is It a Bad Idea?

| Online learning makes sense for organizations when: | Online learning makes sense for learners when: |
| --- | --- |
| People are comfortable using technology for their information and learning needs.<br>Learning access is improved as a result.<br>Learning generally—and technology-based learning specifically—is vocally and visibly supported by key stakeholders and given the resources to succeed. | They want and need to learn this way.<br>They have access to the technology.<br>They have enough time and skills to use the technology.<br>They perceive it as adding value to their work and lives.<br>They have support to help them with technology issues. |
| **Online learning may be a bad idea for organizations when:** | **Online learning may be a bad idea for learners when:** |
| "Everyone else is doing it" is the reason for doing it.<br>It doesn't fit into the organizational culture or processes.<br>Resources and support are insufficient. | They aren't comfortable with technology.<br>They don't have access or time.<br>They need more interaction or support than will be provided.<br>They're unable or unwilling to learn this way. |

Table 1.1 may be somewhat misleading if it makes you think you have to make a cut-and-dried choice between delivering instruction online or in person. The truth is that in many cases, a combination of delivery methods works better than either one on its own. (You'll sometimes hear this called "blended" or "hybrid" learning.) Perhaps it would be easier to think about using technologies for learning on a continuum, from no use of technologies to technologies doing all of the teaching. This continuum is illustrated in Figure 1.1.

No technologies used ⟷ Only technologies used

| Traditional classroom course | Classroom with technologies (video, etc.) | Hybrid course: part classroom, part online | Synchronous online course, with instruction taking place in real time via the Internet | Instructor-led online course with asynchronous discussion | Self-paced learning on CD-ROM or Internet |
|---|---|---|---|---|---|

Figure 1.1. The Technology Continuum

## How Can I Tell Whether My Organization Is Ready?

Most organizations and learners aren't ready from the get-go. But the good news is that contrary to popular belief, lack of readiness is not a big red stop sign for your online learning initiative. Instead, it simply means you have work to do. In some ways, it's like finishing your basement. If you're like me, there's lots of activity (cleaning, buying resources, and so forth) that needs to happen before the drywall goes up. So if you think you have some work ahead of you before getting started, you're right, and that's OK—it's expected, even.

Here are three critical questions I ask when assessing whether an organization is ready to put instruction online:

- *Is the organization ready?* Has your organization budgeted enough for the project? Are the right people with the right skills already available, or will you need to find additional employees or contractors? Does the company have the hardware, software, and technology infrastructure it needs, as well as enough IT support? How will additional resources be gained if needed?
- *Are learners ready?* Do learners have access to the right equipment and software? Do they have the computer

and Internet skills they need to find and use learning materials online? How motivated are they to learn in a new way? What do you need to do to get them on board and ready?

- *Are you ready?* How will you build new skills (we'll talk more about this later in this chapter) and what help will you need?

As an instructional technology consultant who has worked with lots and lots of different organizations, the most important advice I can give is to do your homework and ask the tough questions up front. Take a look at your organization's key business and learning needs and see whether technology makes sense for meeting them. In some cases it will, and in other cases it won't. Then look at potential learners to see what problems you may be creating for them. Fix the problems first, or do something that makes better sense for everyone.

For example, I once worked with a client who needed to train the company's couriers on a new regulation. They didn't want the couriers to miss work, so they decided to develop online learning modules for off-duty drivers. An analysis of the situation showed us that it made much more sense to provide an audio tape (so couriers could listen while driving) and workbook. Building online learning modules didn't make sense; it would have cost a lot and created too many roadblocks.

Although each situation is different, the items in Table 1.2 can provide you with a general assessment of your organization's readiness for online learning. "Yes" answers, of course, are better than "no" answers, but the real question is whether your organization should start moving *toward* online learning. Most organizations have some work to do to get there, so don't feel bad if yours does, too. It's to be expected.

Seems like common sense? It is. You wouldn't buy a sofa to fit a certain spot in your family room without measuring the space first and seeing how it fits with the other furniture. That's what you're

Table 1.2. Are We Ready to Use Technologies for Learning?

|  | | | |
|---|---|---|---|
| Our organization and our people will benefit from using technology for learning. | Yes | ??? | No |
| We have a plan for overall organizational learning, and online learning is integrated into it, not separate from it. | Yes | ??? | No |
| We value learning and developing people for the long run. When resources get tight, we still make learning a high priority. | Yes | ??? | No |
| We gain buy-in and support when introducing changes in our company. | Yes | ??? | No |
| We are willing to invest in changes that we believe are needed, even if they do not pay off immediately. | Yes | ??? | No |
| We are prepared to deal with a complex and changing learning technologies marketplace. | Yes | ??? | No |
| We have the resources (people, time, money) to be successful for the long term. | Yes | ??? | No |
| We have or are willing to adopt and maintain the infrastructure needed for learning technologies. | Yes | ??? | No |
| Our IT people are willing and able to help us succeed. | Yes | ??? | No |
| We have the knowledge and skills to design, develop, and implement learning technologies. | Yes | ??? | No |
| We know what instructional strategies to use to optimize learning and how to use available media to support them. | Yes | ??? | No |
| We know how to find help (resources, consultants, vendors, contractors) that will allow us to be successful for the long run. | Yes | ??? | No |
| People using online learning will receive the level of interaction and support they need. | Yes | ??? | No |
| Learners are comfortable using computers, browsers, and networks to access and share information. | Yes | ??? | No |
| Learners have access to instructional materials delivered through technologies. | Yes | ??? | No |
| Learners have time to use instructional materials delivered through technologies. | Yes | ??? | No |
| Learners are willing to learn this way. | Yes | ??? | No |

doing here: measuring the space, looking for a fit, and thinking about whether it makes sense to buy it at all.

## What Is Good Online Learning?

If you've seen much of what passes for online learning, you may be skeptical about this medium. Too many online courses are nothing but boring page-turners, in which "interactivity" means the learner gets to click on the Next button before snoozing his or her way through a series of quiz questions that most trained chimps could answer correctly.

Part of the reason this has happened is that folks generally imitate old media (poorly) when using a new medium. For instance, when film was a new medium, directors did nothing more than capture stage plays with a movie camera. Over time, they realized that movies didn't have to follow the same rules as stage plays. They began optimizing the best characteristics of the new medium—for example, the fact that you could have unlimited scene changes and add special effects, something you can't do on stage. Voilà! *Star Wars!*

Online learning has followed the same pattern. By designing online courses that were essentially nothing more than textbooks on a computer screen, early developers failed to use the Web's unique advantages to their fullest. What we should be doing instead is evaluating the characteristics of these technologies in order to consider what they are naturally good for. Table 1.3 outlines some of the pros and cons of both classroom and online learning. For example, networks allow people to communicate and share. Consider all the information you send and receive via e-mail. It's an inexpensive and reliable way of sharing your knowledge. The good news is that we can easily harness these capabilities for learning. We will spend some time in this book telling you how to do that.

Different types of content require different kinds of materials and strategies. Teaching someone to follow a well-specified procedure—

Table 1.3. What Are the Pros and Cons of Classroom Learning and Online Learning?

| Potential Pros: Classroom Learning | Potential Cons: Classroom Learning |
|---|---|
| Immediate feedback | Shy or analytical people contribute less |
| Visual cues | Instructor controlled |
| Ease of social interaction | Event based (happens at one specific time) |
| Favors those who communicate well in person | |
| **Potential Pros: Online Learning** | **Potential Cons: Online Learning** |
| Everyone can contribute | Lack of visual cues |
| Learner controlled | Technological and access hurdles |
| Process based (can happen any time, any place) | Favors those who communicate well in writing |
| Permanent record of communication | |

for instance, how to make text bold in Microsoft Word—is an entirely different task from that of teaching folks to make ethical decisions, which involves teaching people how to think rather than just what steps to follow. To teach software skills, a straightforward software simulation with feedback would probably work well. To teach ethics, you'll need some way to delve into lots of messy situations. In other words, learners will need to do activities that require intense reflection and synthesis. You might want them to research ethical situations in the newspaper or react to case studies.

Different types of learners need different types of learning experiences. You might need to train bus drivers how to enter their daily receipts differently than you would train accountants to use a new accounting system. Senior execs probably have different time commitments than customer service reps. Hospital food service workers have different access to computers than the people working in accounts receivable. Undergrads may need a different level of support than graduate students. Good online learning takes into account the needs of the people receiving the instruction.

Lastly, good online learning prepares people to use the online content the same way it's used in the real world. If real-life customers won't be following an exact script when they phone the call center to complain about defective merchandise, for example, why should we train call-center reps to memorize one rigid script? An analysis of how the content is used in the real world needs to precede the design and development of instruction.

## What Skills Do I Need?

One of my best friends, Helen Macfarlane, a gifted medical illustrator and Flash animator who works for the University of Colorado Health Sciences Center in Denver, called me a while back for some advice. She was working on an online course to educate patients about pancreatic cancer and was frustrated with the instructional aspects of the animation. She told me that she wished she had my knowledge of how to make online learning compelling. I laughed out loud and said I'd be thrilled to know how to draw as well as she does. We decided that between the two of us, we had a pretty decent range of skills.

My clients and students often ask me what they need to know in order to develop their own online learning. There's no simple answer. The certificate program I teach covers the basics of instructional design, authoring, animation, graphics, and programming. But even that list of topics doesn't provide everything you need to know; for example, we don't go into great depth on networks and bandwidth—important topics for anyone developing Web-based courses.

As leaders of online learning projects, we do need to know an awful lot. But what exactly does "an awful lot" mean? In order to gain a balanced perspective, I asked some experts what they see as the primary skills needed to design, develop, and facilitate online learning.

Many of us clearly see that our field is changing. "Training and development has become a more complex field than it was ten years ago," says Margaret Driscoll, of IBM Mindspan Solutions in Cambridge, Massachusetts. She says mastering the discipline means knowing and applying the concepts of instructional design, cognitive psychology, and the principles of adult learning. Add to that a host of specialized skills in videography, editing, database design, content authoring, and project management.

"Unlike many traditional classroom programs, it truly takes a cross-functional team to do a good job," she says. For example, someone has to know something about server administration, learning standards, software integration, and usability testing. One lone person can't do all of that well.

Some of my clients mistakenly assume I know everything there is to know about online learning. Because of this, I make sure I'm very clear about which skills I have and which ones I don't. **It's important to be realistic about what you don't know and get the help you need.**

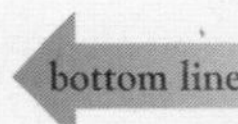


## Design and Development

According to Saul Carliner, assistant professor of educational technology at Concordia University, Montreal, Canada, design means "determining the audience, purpose, and constraints of an online learning program; determining the most appropriate format in which to present the content; and developing high-level and detailed design plans."

These analysis skills are critical, says Maureen Hencmann, instructional designer at Regis University in Denver, because they lay the foundation for your entire online learning effort. It's also important to know how to build rapport with others on the e-learning team, which means finding out what their skills are and deciding how to use those talents to develop a quality product.

Designers also need to be excellent interviewers who know how to talk to subject matter experts. "It's difficult for subject matter experts to describe completely what they know, so designers need to know how to help them," says Kirsti Aho, director of education and e-learning at Macromedia in San Francisco. People who know how to ask good questions can apply this skill to learners, as well. Too often, we don't know who our learners are or what they need, so our courses (and the learners) suffer as a result.

Along with knowing how to interview subject matter experts, online learning designers have to be able to explain complex subjects in simple terms, says William Horton, president of William Horton Consulting in Boulder, Colorado. Although most educators are pretty good speakers and writers, communicating online requires different skills.

For example, most online courses require short, concise blocks of text. Aho recalls the time she wrote what she thought was a great online course, only to have her manager delete at least half the words. "I was appalled and offended," says Aho, "but she was right."

Good e-learning designers also know how to keep the big picture in mind. "Design is not just a rote application of a canned instructional design methodology," says Horton. "It means picking an instructional strategy to suit the goals and learners at hand." In other words, we need to go further than the performance technology skills that many training organizations are recommending. For instance, research shows that learning is essentially a social activity, but there isn't much (or any) attention paid to the social aspects of learning in many of the online courses I see—a shame, since the Internet makes socialization easy.

Once you've designed an online course, the next step is actually creating the material. In order to do that, you need to know something about your users' computers, networks, and media as well as the Internet's capabilities and limitations. You don't have to be an expert on every tool and technology in the industry, but it's important to understand how various tools work.

If that seems like a tall order, start by simply figuring out which tools are best at which tasks. "Many tools can get the job done," says Ken Cline, director of development at Redmon Group in Alexandria, Virginia, "but each tool imposes certain limitations."

### Facilitation

Facilitation skills fall into three categories: facilitating synchronous (live) events, moderating asynchronous discussions, and coaching learners. "A proactive coach sets the energy and tone early on in the course and maintains that momentum throughout," says Roberta Westwood, president of Westwood Dynamics Learning and Development in West Vancouver, British Columbia. "Even a well-designed course can fall apart through inattention on the part of the instructor."

Macromedia's Aho points out that facilitators also need to understand how to work with different types of learners, content, and media. And they need excellent project management skills in order to keep people on track.

### There's More

Already mastered the skills we've talked about? Don't get too comfortable—there are a few more you should put on your list.

You'll want to become more knowledgeable about e-learning standards, learning objects, metadata, and XML. (See Chapter 6.) "This knowledge will become increasingly important for producing e-learning for commercial distribution, or for an organization that wants to build e-learning content that can be easily searched and accessed," says Carol Fallon, president of Integrity eLearning in Anaheim Hills, California. She's right: I can tell you from my own experience that this knowledge has become more and more critical in the past six months.

Another area you might want to study: accessibility. Virtually any work performed for the U.S. federal government, for example, requires some accessibility compliance and analysis. Plus you'll want to be sure disabled viewers can learn from your instructional materials as easily as anyone else.

## How Do I Stay Sane?

This is a crazy, fast-changing field, and it's a bit of a struggle to learn and stay current. But we're not the only ones. My accountant complains about annual changes to tax law and my mechanic tells me Subarus are getting so complex he's going to need an advanced computer science engineering degree to keep current. I guess that means we're all part of the expanding knowledge society and should be proud that we're so smart!

If you're new to this field, you may feel overwhelmed by the number of things to learn and relearn. That's to be expected, but I'd like to let you in on a secret. Everyone in this field—at least those who are being honest with themselves—has felt that way and still feels that way.

bottom line

The best route is right in front of you. **Jump in, start somewhere, and be prepared to keep learning.** Prioritize the things you need to learn and start with the most important. I often advise my clients and students to get out on the Web and take online courses. There are thousands of free samples available—some good and some awful. Analyze them, critique them, and figure out what works and what doesn't. Instructional sites often lag behind those dedicated to e-commerce and marketing, so look at sites that have nothing to do with education and figure out what lessons you can apply to online learning.

The good news is that it's loads of fun. Read books, attend conferences, ask questions, join professional organizations, take courses, and keep smiling. I figure if my accountant and mechanic can keep up with changes in their fields, who am I to complain too loudly? (Complaining softly, on the other hand, is just fine.)

Welcome to this field. The fact that you're new is a major plus, in my opinion. What's been done up until now is far from stellar—we need fresh eyes and some new blood!

## Resources

See the companion Web site for this book, http://www.learningpeaks.com/msoll/, for links to resources that will help you take the next steps to becoming more expert in this field.

# 2

# What About Learning?

Consider the tragedy that can result when a police officer doesn't know much about human behavior. Or the potentially deadly consequences of a civil engineer not understanding how to properly apply scientific laws of force and gravity when building a bridge. For every type of expertise, there are fundamental skills and knowledge. Just as the laws of physics are critical to the designs of a civil engineer, how people learn is fundamental to the design of good instruction in any medium.

If you don't have a background in how people learn, it's extremely important to read this chapter. (It might be a decent refresher if you already have some knowledge in this area, too.) I teach new instructional developers at a university and in numerous corporate training departments, and I've seen firsthand how erroneous notions about learning can negatively affect people and organizations. Having some knowledge about how people learn is truly critical to your success and the success of the folks who will be using your instructional materials.

In this chapter we'll answer the following questions:

- What is learning?
- What is instruction?
- What activities should be included in instruction?

## What Is Learning?

My son used to be a Lego fanatic. He was obsessed with how things fit together. We'd try to get him to eat dinner or watch a movie with the family, but he was often too absorbed in what he was doing. In school, when teachers requested drawings, his were always three-dimensional with cross-sections. No one told him to learn these things or provided him with a formal curriculum; he had an internal passion and learned these skills without any formal course of study. No instructional designers, instructors, or assessment.

We've all experienced learning this way. My husband's excellent photography skills were gained primarily through self-study and practice. I learned Web development through a combination of courses and obsessive trial and error. One of my friends, a fabulous art quilter, gained her skills over years of intense study and practice.

John Holt, once a fifth grade teacher and visiting lecturer at Harvard and Berkeley, went on to became a famous advocate for alternate forms of schooling. In an interview reprinted in *The Natural Child Project* Web site (www.naturalchild.com/guest/marlene_bumgarner.html), he said, "The human animal is a learning animal; we like to learn; we need to learn; we are good at it; we don't need to be shown how or made to do it. What kills the processes are the people interfering with it or trying to regulate it or control it."

Holt provides us with essential truths about learning. Learning is a natural process. Human beings want to learn and are built to deal with the frustrations inherent in learning. You and I can interfere with this natural learning process, but it would be far better to work with it than against it. So let's think about how we learn and how we can use this knowledge to facilitate, not work against, learning.

### Learning as Transmitting Information

Here's one view of how we learn: The instructor (or trainer or expert) wishes to transmit information to the learners. The process looks something like that shown in Figure 2.1.

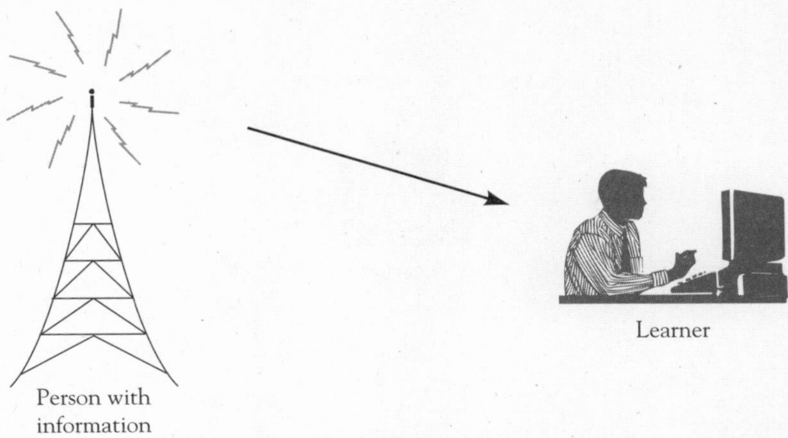


Figure 2.1. Transmission View of Learning

The learners acquire information from the expert and add it to their memory. Table 2.1. shows some learning elements and their role in learning according to this view.

Table 2.1. Transmission View: Learning Elements and Their Role in Learning

| Elements | Role in Learning |
|---|---|
| Expert, instructor | Determine what information needs to be transmitted to learners |
| Designer, developer | Present information so the learner can acquire it |
| Learner | Receiver of information |
| Content | Information to be transmitted |
| Learning activities | Opportunities to assess recall |
| Technologies | Present content efficiently to facilitate transmission |

## Learning as Constructing Understanding

A contrasting view is that learning is a process that occurs as people actively work to make sense of new information. In this view, learners struggle with new information. They try to figure out what

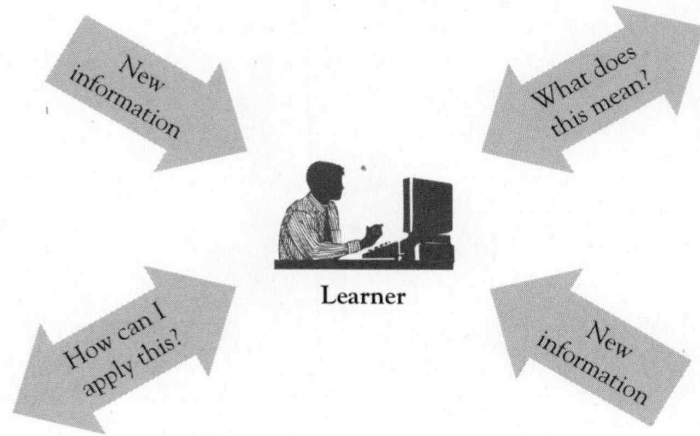


Figure 2.2. Construction View of Learning

it means, how it fits into what they already know, and how to apply it. The process looks something like that shown in Figure 2.2.

In this view, learning is the process of constructing knowledge. It's a continuous and messy process because we are constantly struggling with the meaning of new information and determining how it applies to our lives.

bottom line

**Here's the bottom line on what we're doing when we construct knowledge in this way: We are working to gain expertise, not just to remember isolated facts.** In this view of learning (see Table 2.2.), the learning elements are the same ones as in Table 2.1, but their role in learning is vastly different.

Here's an example of this approach. Recently, I realized I needed to become more expert at using electronic spreadsheets because I was tired of tracking student grades, indoor painting costs, holiday gifts, and so on with just paper and pen. I booted up the spreadsheet software and started to learn. To apply my learning to a current need, I decided to set up a spreadsheet to track grades. In my old pen-and-paper system, I'd keep notes about what kind of help each

Table 2.2. Construction View: Learning Elements and Their Role in Learning

| Elements | Role in Learning |
|---|---|
| Expert, instructor | Uncover the content and processes behind expertise |
| Designer, developer | Design learning opportunities that will help people gain expertise |
| Learner | Constructor and applier of knowledge |
| Content | Part of toolset for gaining expertise |
| Learning activities | Opportunities to gain expertise |
| Technologies | Support for learning activities and expertise |

student needed (problems, misconceptions, and so on). Could I create a field for this item? I jumped around in the book and help screens to figure out how to add and format this text field. I struggled at times with formatting the columns and making the formulas work, but I succeeded.

Sound familiar? There wasn't much transmission of information from the book or help files to my head. I didn't need to memorize a list of facts about the spreadsheet software, but I did need to know how to use the software to meet my needs. Even though I didn't attend a formal class, I was learning—I was making sense of the software and the book, considering how my new knowledge fit with what I already knew, and applying it to a problem I needed to solve.

Both views have some validity. The transferring information view makes some sense for rote memorization and simple objective skills. I can show you, for instance, how to turn on your car's lights and then you can do exactly what I did and succeed in turning the lights on.

The knowledge construction view takes into consideration the need to be able to *use* what you learned, not just remember it.

Turning on your car lights is a simple skill, but driving the car is a complex one. You learn it, like other complex skills, by struggling with new knowledge, seeing how it fits with what you already know, and determining how to apply it.

Think about what you want people to be able to do as a result of using the online materials you develop. If you want them to be able to use and apply (rather than just remember), chances are you want them to be active constructors of knowledge.

## What Is Instruction?

If you believe that learning is primarily transmission of information, the point of instruction is to present information and then see whether learners remember it. If you believe that learning is primarily construction of knowledge, the point of instruction is to create opportunities for learners to gain expertise and then see whether they can use the knowledge in real life. **In most cases, the purpose of instruction is to provide opportunities for learning to occur.**

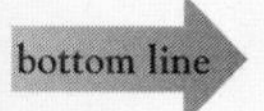


What kinds of things do we want people to learn? Table 2.3 shows the categories of knowledge we often wish to help people construct and examples of each.

Think about *how* we learn about these categories of knowledge. We can learn facts through drill and practice (the transmission method), but we gain most of our knowledge by doing something, getting feedback (consequences, reactions, and so forth), and trying again.

For example, consider learning geometry or algebra. If you only learned how to solve isolated problems (the way many of us were taught), chances are you cannot apply it very well in everyday life. Learning theorists call this kind of knowledge "inert"—it's relatively useless to us because we don't know how to use it in context.

Let's take this idea one step further and look at what kinds of activities we can add to our instruction to be sure learners' knowledge isn't inert.

Table 2.3. Categories of Knowledge

| Categories of Knowledge | Examples |
|---|---|
| Facts: discrete pieces of data such as names, dates, times | Dates to send in tax payments<br>Post office location |
| Concepts: umbrella ideas and the essential characteristics that define them and distinguish them from others | Geometry<br>Computer networks |
| Principles: rules, guidelines, criteria to drive decision making and actions | Writing defensible performance appraisals<br>Rubric for developing a Web site that is easy to use |
| Procedures: how-tos, step-by-step tasks | How to attach a file to an e-mail message<br>How to write a receipt |
| Processes: progression of events | Hiring process<br>Circulatory process |
| Structures: what something is made up of | Parts of a toilet<br>Sections of a dissertation |

The information above was adapted from Information Mapping's Information Types (www.infomap.com).

## What Activities Should Be Included in Instruction?

Now that we know we need to create opportunities for learners to construct knowledge, we need to consider how to develop instructional materials that are likely to make this occur. We do this primarily through interactions and activities that allow learners to struggle with the content, fit it into their existing knowledge, and apply it to the kinds of problems they face in the real world.

Too many online courses consist of content and not much else. That's because the transmission view of learning is so prevalent.

The truth is that content is necessary, but it's not enough. What's missing is meaningful interaction and activities. (And yes, omitting interaction is easier to do online than in person, but let's be fair. I remember plenty of my own in-person learning experiences that had less-than-optimal interaction. Remember lecture courses of three hundred students taught by a teaching assistant?)

Interaction occurs when the learner has to *do* something and gets meaningful feedback in return. Yeah, clicking on the Next button is "doing something," but it doesn't fulfill the definition because nothing meaningful happens as a result. The learner needs to interact with content, people, or the technology itself to make something happen, get feedback and input, and learn from the experience.

How did you learn to walk? By interacting with the world around you (the rug, the table edge), making mistakes, refining your efforts, and trying again. How will you learn to make ethical business decisions? Probably not by answering multiple-choice questions on a screen.

This may seem like common sense. Research shows, however, that much traditionally designed instruction doesn't transfer well to real-life settings. What makes knowledge and skills "stick" is using them the same way you'd use them in the real world. Multiple choice is not the way most of us deal with the world. (Life would be easier if it were—I'd be right 25 percent of the time even when I didn't have a clue!)

If interaction is important, how do we make it occur? Table 2.4 gives a few examples. I've provided two columns of activities in order to highlight the difference between activities that promote remembering (for example, naming countries that start with A) and those that promote the ability to *use* the content in real-life situations. Please note that the activities listed could fall into another category if used in a different way.

Table 2.4. Interaction Types and Related Activities

| Interaction Types | Activities That Promote Recall | Activities That Require Higher-Level Thinking |
|---|---|---|
| Interaction with content (text, video, graphics, simulations, programming) | JavaScript quiz<br>Drill-and-practice<br>Learning games<br>Flash cards<br>Simple animation<br>Glossary<br>Presentation sequence (text-graphics or slides-text)<br>FAQs | Pre-work<br>Tutorial<br>Hands-on practice<br>Field work<br>Simulation<br>Guided analysis<br>Virtual lab<br>Field trip<br>Scavenger hunt<br>Job aid<br>Journaling, reflection |
| Interaction with people (other learners, subject matter experts, instructors, etc.) | One-way Webcast (instructor to students)<br>FAQs<br>Group test preparation | Pre-work<br>Case study<br>Document review<br>Build model<br>Build lesson<br>Peer review, group critique<br>Team design<br>Team discussion<br>Build resource list<br>Role play<br>Position paper<br>Journaling, reflection |
| Interaction with technology | Site map<br>Help files<br>FAQs | Tutorials<br>Demos<br>Help desk |

## How Do I Select Interactions and Activities?

You're standing on a beautiful mountain slope and the ski instructor is showing your beginners' group how to point the tips of your skis together in a snowplow technique. After she's done explaining, you give it a try and end up careening sideways into a fellow group member. You dust yourself off and try again. And again. After a while, you sort of get the hang of it. Eventually, you try using this skill on a more advanced slope.

Perhaps you've already read a book about skiing, or maybe you even took a short online course. Both are helpful. But nothing replaces trying things out and dealing with the realities of the situation (steep hills, icy slopes, the constant need to blow your nose) to make it hit home.

Let's see how this applies to an online course.

Let's say your boss e-mails you with a heads-up about a new course development project. She's been given the OK to forge ahead with the online performance management course your group has been pitching and wants to know what the first step is. (Performance management, for those outside the training and human resources world, is a term for how supervisors plan, track, and assess behavior and job contributions. A performance management course, then, would be likely to teach best practices for managing these events.)

If your answer to your boss is, "Figure out what topics need to be taught," you'd be on familiar curriculum development ground, but you'd be wide of the mark. A better place to start is to ask yourself what people actually need to *do* with that content in their real-life jobs. It may be a subtle difference, but it makes *all* the difference.

This is a drastic shift in thinking about what we're doing when we design instruction. The old way of thinking was simply, "I need to teach these topics." A better way of thinking is "I need to help learners get the knowledge and skills they'll need in the real world. My job is to improve their expertise."

Let's apply this new way of thinking to our performance management course. Instead of developing a list of topics and then looking for content to "cover" those topics, you learn how the process operates in real life and see how experienced managers and human resources personnel deal with performance management issues. Once you know what those issues are, you design course activities that will help managers learn how to prevent or solve these typical problems.

Using the example above, Table 2.5 shows the categories of knowledge and how they apply to your performance management course.

Table 2.5. Categories of Knowledge Applied to Performance Management Course

| Categories of Knowledge | Application to Performance Management Knowledge and Skills |
|---|---|
| Facts: discrete pieces of data like names, dates, times | Deadlines for completing forms<br>Human resources people who can help |
| Concepts: umbrella ideas and the essential characteristics that define them and distinguish them from others | Performance management |
| Principles: rules, guidelines, criteria to drive decision making and actions | Writing performance plans<br>Handling typical performance problems<br>Providing performance feedback<br>Writing defensible performance appraisals |
| Procedures: how-tos, step-by-step tasks | Entering performance data into HR system |
| Processes: progression of events | Yearly performance management cycle |
| Structures: what something is made up of | Parts of a performance appraisal and how it's organized |

Now it's time to develop the course activities. Let's say that one typical problem is that managers don't know how to equitably deal with employee absences. Experienced practitioners tell you they deal with this problem by consulting the employee policy manual, discussing situations with human resources personnel, carefully documenting absences, and having discussions with staff. If this situation is handled well, many potential problems (people getting fired, other employees getting angry about a coworker's frequent absences, important work not getting done) are reduced or eliminated.

So how do you design instruction that helps learners gain expertise in appropriately handling employee absences? In Table 2.6, I have provided some ideas. You can probably think of others. The questions are adapted from Dr. Joanna Dunlap's (2003) Problems of Practice method, and the process comes from the in-depth training I regularly do with instructors and designers.

As you look more closely at the interactions and activities I put in Table 2.6, you may wonder whether learners have to do work outside of the actual online course. The answer is yes—remember, an online course doesn't have to be (and, in many cases, shouldn't be) completely online. For instance, you might want learners to build documentation and then get feedback on it from their HR representative. Since managers solve employee performance problems by dealing with people, you'll probably want to build in interpersonal interactions.

bottom line

**How does instruction developed from this point of view differ from coming up with a list of topics and figuring out how to present them? It's more meaningful for learners because the instruction is designed to help them construct knowledge and use it in the real world.** It helps them gain expertise in the actual use of the content, not in just the content itself.

The results are often spectacular. For example, I recently worked with a training department that had developed many online courses for staff and wanted to begin developing some for outside clients.

Table 2.6. Suggested Course Activities

| Question to Ask | Suggested Instructional Interactions and Activities for an Online Course |
|---|---|
| **What is the real-life challenge?** Some managers don't know how to deal equitably with employee absences. If they handle this inequitably, they harm employees and put the company at risk. | Build a case study that allows learners to realistically deal with the challenge. Designers can build these cases or learners can develop cases that relate to their work.<br>Facilitate a discussion about unfair circumstances managers have dealt with in their careers. |
| **What knowledge and skills do experienced practitioners have to prevent or solve this challenge?** Experienced practitioners understand the importance of fairness and equity and the potentially damaging results of inequity. They know what the policy is on employee absences, follow that policy similarly for all employees, document their actions, and gain help from HR as needed. | Have learners build a flowchart of potential steps and decisions at each step.<br>Bring manuals and documentation to the training. Ask learners to read these manuals and come up with a list of questions for their HR rep about what they've read.<br>Assessment: Ask learners to develop an actual document to track absences (rather than giving them a multiple-choice quiz about documenting absences). |

The problem with the existing courses, I told them (gingerly), was that the learner didn't have to do anything meaningful. The courses could just as easily have been downloadable PDF documents—and learners probably would have been happier because they wouldn't have had to read large quantities of text on the screen. I worked with the client using the process described here to build three new courses that taught learners how to use the content in the way it would be used in the real world. On our final workshop day, one client came in to evaluate these courses and was thrilled by how useful they were.

## Conclusion

Learning isn't about pouring information into learners' heads so they can remember facts or do simple skills. It's about helping people struggle with how to make personal sense of what they are learning and apply it to real situations. Our mission is to figure out what learners need to be able to do in real life and then design instruction that helps them do those things. If they're able to successfully answer multiple-choice questions about a certain job-related task but don't know how to actually *do* the task once they leave the course and go back to work, we haven't done our jobs.

# 3

# The Language of Online Learning

## *How to Spell HTML*

When I was hired as head of health education and training for a health care organization many moons ago, I began playing around with different ways of using technology to teach staff and patients. I soon realized that although I knew a lot about training, I needed to understand the technical side of things better. I studied, did research, and asked lots of questions about topics such as networks and programming. Before long, I heard comments like, "Let's discuss the bandwidth and server requirements of what I'm proposing" and "What kind of impact on network operations are we looking at?" coming out of my mouth when I talked to network administrators. This allowed me to be on speaking terms with the folks in the information technology (IT) department—a good thing!

This chapter will address one very important question: What are the most common (mostly technical) terms that are misunderstood by folks new to this field, and what do they mean?

### How to Speak the Right Language

If you want to design and develop online learning, surely you've had the nagging feeling that you don't know enough about technology. It could be that the systems folks blew you off when you made what you considered to be a perfectly harmless request. Perhaps the network administrator sneered at a proposal that she said would slow down the whole network. Why are these folks so mean and hard to get along with? Truth is, they're not. They just know things that we non-techies generally don't. If we're using technology to teach, we need to be able to get along with IT. And as instructional project managers and potential consumers of technical products (authoring tools, LMSs, and so forth), we need to be able to speak the right language.

If you're not convinced, consider this scenario. Some time ago, I realized that my Web hosting service (the organization that rents server space for Web sites and provides access to them to the rest of the world) wasn't meeting my needs. So I started looking around at alternatives. The fact that I had a decent understanding of server technologies made the choices pretty clear. I was able to ask the right questions, and they didn't peg me as a dumber-than-dirt type who could be sold the world.

bottom line

**Some folks say this stuff is way too complicated for someone without a computer science or engineering degree, but that's simply not true.** Here are my three steps for learning geek speak:

1. *Attitude shift*. You have to see a need for learning technical concepts and decide to make the effort.
2. *Start somewhere*. Pick an area and start looking for understandable information (on the Web, in books like this one, in classes). Start with the companion Web site for this book, http://www.learningspeaks.com/msoll/.
3. *Fill in the gaps*. As you learn, you'll begin to figure out what else you don't know and you can go from there. Everything you learn makes the next step easier.

I promise that it's quite do-able, especially in small "bytes."

## What Are the Most Common Terms That Are Misunderstood by Folks New to This Field, and What Do They Mean?

A preliminary step for many folks who are new to this world is to gain a handle on the jargon. In this chapter, we'll present simple explanations for some of the most commonly used terms. After that, it'll be time to go a little deeper into what the technology does. (See Chapters 5 and 6.)

*Accessibility*

*Accessibility* refers to ease of access for people with disabilities. Accessible Web sites can be easily used by those with visual, hearing, motor, or cognitive impairments.

Accessibility is not only the right thing to do—it also makes good business sense. Section 508 of the U.S. Government 1998 Rehabilitation Act says that all electronic and information technology procured, used, or developed by the federal government must be accessible to people with disabilities. Because of that, many e-learning vendors are developing accessible learning materials for their government and nongovernment clients.

*AICC*

*AICC* stands for the Aviation Industry CBT Committee. The group first came together to develop guidelines for the aviation industry for the development, delivery, and evaluation of CBT (computer-based training) and other training technologies. Although AICC originally developed its standards for the aviation industry, these specifications have been at the forefront of the learning standards movement.

The term *AICC compliant* means that a training product complies with one or more of the AICC Guidelines and Recommendations (AGRs). There are nine AGRs, so AICC compliance can mean a number of different things. To make sure you know exactly what you're getting, you may want to ask, "Which AGRs do you comply with?" when vendors tout AICC compliance.

### *Asynchronous*

*Asynchronous* learning means people use the instructional materials and technologies at different times. Learners communicate with each other and the instructor, but it's a back-and-forth discussion rather than a "synchronous" real-time class or meeting.

Examples include e-mail, threaded discussions, most higher-education online courses, and self-paced online courses. Advantages are convenience, accessibility, time to think before communicating, and lack of visual cues (learners can't make incorrect assumptions based on visual cues). Disadvantages include lack of visual cues (learners don't have visual cues to help them understand people's intent) and lack of immediacy.

### *Authoring*

*Authoring* means developing instructional materials by using tools, course management systems, or programming. Some *authoring tools* are specifically made for instructional use. Others are more generic and can be used for any type of Web authoring.

Dreamweaver (Figure 3.1), Flash, and Lectora are examples of authoring tools, while Blackboard and eCollege are examples of course management systems. HTML, JavaScript, and PHP are programming languages.

### *Bandwidth*

*Bandwidth* is a measure of how fast data move on a given transmission path (phone lines, network cables, and so forth). It's measured in the amount of data transmitted per second (bits or bytes per second—bps or Bps). The more data that can be moved, the higher the bandwidth.

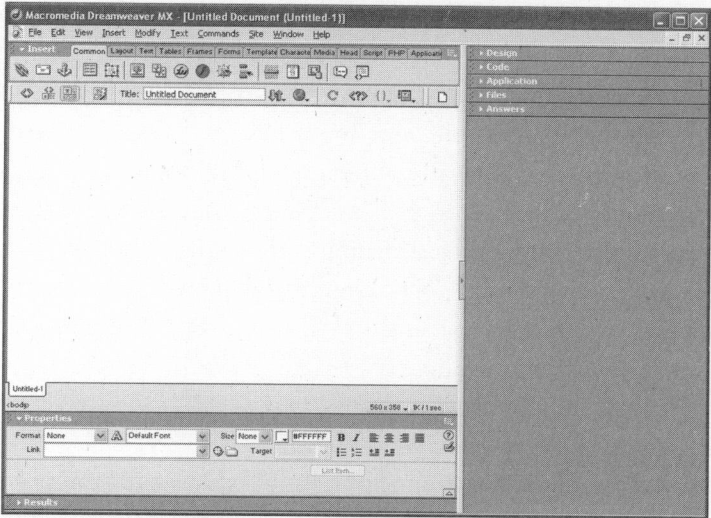


Figure 3.1. Dreamweaver MX Authoring Tool

Bandwidth is determined by the transmission media. Data move more quickly through a network cable, for example, than through a phone line—in much the same way water runs through a drain pipe faster than it does through a straw. Some people refer to transmission media as "pipes." Those that move small amounts of data are considered small pipes; those that can move large amounts of data are big pipes.

Bandwidth also depends on the complexity of the data moving through the "pipes." For example, video is generally more complex than a photograph, and a photograph is more complex than a text file. The more complex the data, the more bandwidth is needed.

A dial-up connection using a phone line (equivalent to the straw example above) is a low-bandwidth connection. Higher bandwidth is most often provided by cable modems, DSL, and T-1 lines.

### *Blended or Hybrid Learning*

*Blended* or *hybrid learning* refers to a combination of learning methods (including, but not limited to, online and face-to-face instruction). For example, you might have a course in which students learn the basics in an online module and then meet in person for an in-depth discussion of the concepts they've learned online. The advantage of blended learning is that it uses the best features of each delivery method—for example, the immediate feedback that happens in classroom learning and the self-paced exploration that's possible in online learning.

### *Database*

*Databases* store electronic content and deliver it in response to a user request. If a user makes a selection from a drop-down list, types text into a text box, or selects a specific graphic from a list of thumbnail (small) graphics, a request goes to the database to get the desired content (text, pictures, streaming audio clips, Flash movies, and so forth) and bring it to the user (Figure 3.2). A major advantage of databases is that they can hold a large amount of content, which users can sort and search through according to their own needs.

### *DHTML*

*Dynamic HTML* is a general term for HTML markup tags that allow you to create more engaging Web content than is possible with older HTML tags alone. For example, Web pages with the following functionality probably use dynamic HTML:

- Images that change when you roll your mouse over them
- "Dragging and dropping" an image from one place to another on a Web page

One problem with using DHTML is that its functionalities are not supported by all browsers equally. Therefore, it's critical to know

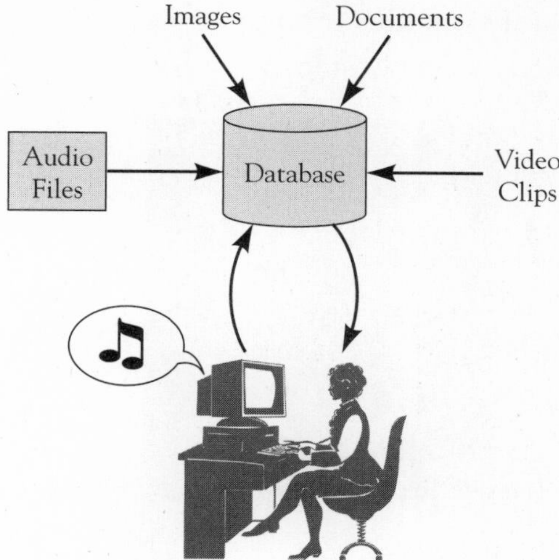


Figure 3.2. Learner Asking for and Receiving an Audio File from a Web Database

what browsers your learners are using in order to make sure they can access DHTML-created content.

*Distance Learning or Online Learning*

The best definition I've found for *distance learning* is "planned learning that normally occurs in a different place from teaching and as a result, requires special techniques of course design, special instructional techniques, special methods of communication by electronic and other technology, as well as special organizational and administrative arrangements" (Moore & Kearsley, 1996, p. 2).

*Online learning* is a form of distance learning that uses network technologies, most commonly the Internet or an intranet.

*GIFs and JPEGs*

These are the two most commonly used graphic formats on the Web. They're generally highly compressed (electronically reduced in size) so they download quickly.

*GIF* stands for Graphics Interchange Format. This type of graphic file is used for simple drawings or line art (Figure 3.3).

Figure 3.3. This Is a GIF Image from a Web Site I Developed

*JPEG or JPG* (pronounced jay-peg) stands for Joint Photographic Experts Group. This type of graphic file is used for complex illustrations or pictures (Figure 3.4).

Figure 3.4. This Is a JPEG Image from My Site

### *Granularity*

*Granularity* relates to size or scale. More granular means smaller in scale. This term is a common one in fields such as astronomy and photography. In online learning, people use the term when they talk about reusing a piece of learning content. For example, a photo is likely to be more granular (more easily reused) than a half-hour video or sixteen-slide PowerPoint presentation. The less granular the original object is, the more work you'll need to do to adapt it to new uses.

*HTML*

*HMTL* (Hypertext Markup Language) consists of "markup codes" that are inserted into a file. These codes tell the file how it will look in a Web browser.

This is some HTML code:

<bold>This is bold text.</bold>

This is how that HTML looks in a Web browser:

**This is bold text.**

*Interaction or Interactivity*

*Interaction* influences learning by causing the learner to do, think, or react. Interaction provides a means for feedback during the learning process. At the very minimum, instructional interaction requires that a learner's efforts result in some kind of response.

Interaction can be with people (other learners, an instructor, a mentor) or with content (interactive forms, animations, simulations). Certain interactions are more meaningful, and therefore more useful, for learning.

*Interface*

An *interface* consists of cues (mostly visual) that tell us how to use something. On a VCR, the interface is the array of buttons, slots, and knobs. On a door, it's the placement of the handle, hinges, and text such as PUSH HERE. On the Web, an interface consists of the images, text, and placement of items on the screen that tell users how to navigate. (If it's hard to use, that means the interface is badly designed.)

### *Interoperability*

*Interoperability* is the ability of content and systems to work with other content and systems. For learning-related content, this generally means that content you develop to work in one type of online learning infrastructure, such as a learning management system (LMS), will also work in another. Interoperability is the goal of groups like SCORM that are attempting to come up with learning standards.

### *JavaScript and Java*

*JavaScript* is a Web programming language that provides more functionality than simple HTML programming. Whereas HTML primarily formats text and images, JavaScript lets you program pop-up messages, new browser windows, feedback when users click on a button, and images (often buttons) that change when users roll their mouse over them. JavaScript can be embedded in the programming of a Web page along with HTML codes.

This is some JavaScript:

```
<a href="discussions.html" onMouseover=
"document.discuss_button.src='discuss_down.jpg'"
onMouseout="document.discuss_button.src='discuss_up.jpg'"><i
mg src="discuss_up.jpg" name="discuss_button" alt="Discussion"
width="120" height="40" border="0"></a>
```

This is how that JavaScript looks in a Web browser before the mouse rolls over it:

This is how the button looks after the mouse rolls over it:

The coding may look confusing, but what it's doing is substituting one image for another when the user places his or her mouse over the original image. Authoring tools such as Dreamweaver can create much of this code—you don't have to program it yourself.

By the way, JavaScript isn't the same thing as *Java*, which is a complex stand-alone programming language.

### *LCMS*

*LCMS* stands for learning content management system. These applications manage learning content, including searches, content conversion, and tailored delivery. Content in an LCMS generally consists of learning objects. The goal of an LCMS is to make it possible to reuse learning objects for a variety of learning purposes.

Some LCMSs integrate the capabilities of an LMS (see below) and some include authoring capabilities.

### *Learning Objects*

*Learning objects* are digital media elements (text, graphics, audio, video, animations, and so forth) that can be put together to form lessons, modules, or courses, then reused for other learning purposes. For example, an online new-hire orientation might include a module on policies, pictures of corporate officers, and a scavenger hunt in which learners have to search the company intranet to figure out where different corporate functions are housed. Each of these digital media elements is a learning object that might be used in other courses. For example, the pictures of corporate officers might be reused on an intranet page that allows staff to click on the photos to find out more about each officer's department.

### *LMS*

An *LMS*, or learning management system, is an application that handles administrative tasks such as creating course catalogs, registering users, tracking users within courses, recording data (such as test scores) about learners, and providing reports about users.

### *Metadata*

*Metadata* is data that provides information about other data. For example, metadata about a learning object may include information about the author, topic, file size, keywords, and so on. Learning objects use metadata (which is included in the programming for that learning object) so you can easily find the object by searching an LCMS or other database. The purpose of metadata is to facilitate reusability and interoperability.

### *Monitor Resolution*

*Monitor resolution* refers to the number of horizontal dots (pixels) multiplied by the number of vertical dots (pixels) on a computer monitor. It's a measure of how much information can be displayed on the screen.

Different users will have different monitor resolutions, browsers, systems, and platforms. An important goal of page design is to make Web sites viewable by as many visitors as possible, despite these differences. In many cases, designers choose a resolution of 800 × 600 because it's often the lowest common denominator and is also viewable by most laptops. Pages designed for lower monitor resolution are viewable by monitors set to higher resolution.

### *MPEG*

MPEG (pronounced em-peg) stands for Moving Picture Experts Group. It's a standard for compressing digital audio and video files. When you use this format, you lose some of the file's quality but end up with a much smaller file size. Smaller file sizes are important for transmitting audio and video files over the Web, because they take up less bandwidth than larger files.

*Open-Source*

*Open-source* means the software's source code (the programming code that makes it run) is available to other programmers, who can modify and redistribute it. Linux is an example of widely used and robust open-source software. There are also a number of open-source learning applications.

Open-source software has several advantages. When you have the source code, you don't have to worry about the company that developed it going out of business (a mighty big concern in this field). In addition, it can be modified to meet any organization's needs. Open-source software also tends to be more robust and stable because it's regularly updated by the programming community.

*Plug-in or Player*

A *plug-in* or *player* is an application that allows the browser to play additional multimedia files. Examples of authoring programs that require the viewers to have plug-ins are Flash, Authorware, Quicktime, and Real Media.

Plug-ins give users access to more multimedia files but are often frowned upon by corporate IT departments, because downloading and installing them involves potential security and support problems. Many IT departments provide approved plug-ins though an intranet site or load them on users' computers.

*Prototype*

In this field, we use the term *prototype* to refer to a starting model of an instructional product. Prototypes usually show the interface, navigational elements, graphic design, and some content—in other words, how the final product will look and feel. Prototypes help designers and developers gain feedback in order to design a better product.

*Scalability*

*Scalability* describes how well computer hardware or software functions when usage increases or decreases. If you bought an LMS for a hundred employees but wanted it to work well for a thousand employees (for instance, in the event of a merger), you'd need to make sure you purchased a *scalable* system.

The term is also used to describe how something performs when it's increased or decreased in size. For example, scalable fonts can be made smaller or larger without losing quality.

*SCORM*

*SCORM*, or Shareable Content Object Reference Model, is a federal government specification for technology-based courseware. SCORM guidelines provide a foundation for how the Department of Defense builds and uses technology-based courseware. They have become a widespread standard for corporate and academic use as well. The goal is to create reusable and interoperable content that can run on any online learning infrastructure, such as a learning management system.

*Streaming Media*

*Streaming media* refers to audio or video files that can be played as they are being downloaded so you don't have to wait for the entire file to download first. This functionality requires a streaming media player (a plug-in).

*Synchronous*

*Synchronous* learning means people are using instructional materials at the same time as other learners, even though they may be in different locations. Learners are communicating with each other (or the instructor) in real time.

Examples are chat, audio-conferencing, and video-conferencing. Advantages are instant feedback and visual cues. Disadvantages are logistics and inconvenience, because everyone has to be available at the same time. This can be especially difficult when learners are in different time zones.

*Threaded Discussion*

*Threaded discussion* is an asynchronous communication tool that allows people to communicate and share ideas. The initial posting (message) and replies to that posting are often referred to as a *thread*.

*Usability*

*Usability* is a measure of how easily a person can use a site to achieve his or her goals. Good usability implies low frustration and the ability to do common tasks without excessive effort. *Usability testing* means bringing together small groups of users and watching as they use your site to accomplish specific goals. Once you've done usability testing, you can improve your site's ease of use by making changes in the places where users struggled.

*Web-Safe Color*

*Web-safe color* refers to 216 colors that will display without dithering on any platform (Mac, PC, Unix, and so on) at any resolution (Figure 3.5). *Dithering* is the process of attempting to create a color not in the palette by mixing the available colors from the palette.

*XML*

*eXtensible Markup Language* offers a way to share data across dissimilar formats. Both XML and HTML contain symbols (known as markup tags) that describe aspects of a document. HTML describes

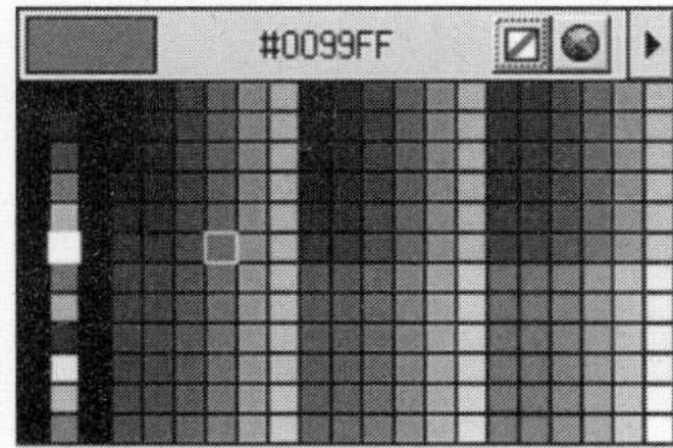


Figure 3.5. Web-Safe Color Palette from Dreamweaver MX

how the data is formatted. For example, the HTML tag <br> places a line break where the tag is placed. XML describes what the data is. So <author> might refer to data about the author of the document. *Extensible* (the X in XML) means it is possible to add new markup tags as they are needed. HTML is not extensible; the available markup tags are already specified.

## New Terms and Technologies

Since this field changes so quickly, the language we use to describe it has to change rapidly, too. It's entirely possible that some new technologies (and terms to describe them) will have appeared on the scene by the time this book goes to print—that's the nature of online learning. Use this blank chart to add new terms and technologies you learn about as you get more involved in online learning—or jot down new acronyms you hear so you can remember to look them up later.

| Term | What Does It Mean? |
| --- | --- |
| | |
| | |
| | |
| | |
| | |
| | |
| | |
| | |
| | |
| | |
| | |
| | |
| | |
| | |
| | |

## Conclusion

As a newcomer to online learning, you may feel like old-timers speak a secret language that you'll never understand. The truth is that every field has its own language (think about medicine, engineering, or art), and online learning is no different. **Because this field encompasses so many different areas—from instructional design to Web programming—we need to be able to talk intelligently about all of those disciplines when we talk about online learning.** As incomprehensible as the jargon may seem right now, though, all you have to do is have an open mind and willingness to learn, and you'll soon be talking about MPEGs, SCORM, and LCMSs with the best of them. This book will help, too: Chapters 4 through 7 will build on the brief definitions we've given you in this chapter.

See the companion Web site for this book, http://www.learningpeaks.com/msoll/, for links to resources that will help you take the next steps to becoming more expert in this field.

# 4

# Designing for the Web

When you visit a Web site, the first thing you notice is what it looks like. Next, you notice whether you're able to find what you need. As you begin to use the site's features, you form opinions about whether it's easy to use. Ultimately, these impressions coalesce into an overall opinion about the site's worth and credibility.

Strangely enough, many sites aren't easy to use. For example, the other day I filled out a Web form to get more information on a car I'd like to buy. When I clicked Submit, I got an error message telling me I'd neglected to fill in my e-mail address. I went back to the form, which didn't have a space to enter an e-mail address. This was a Fortune 500 Web site, and it was unusable.

Designing online instructional materials requires insights from various fields of study, including instructional design, information design, interaction design, and graphic design. That's why so many Web sites are built by a team of people. Even if you don't have a team, it's quite possible to learn how to build effective and usable sites.

In this chapter, we'll build on information about adult learning from Chapter 2. We'll then start looking at some design elements that make online learning materials effective, using the following questions as a guideline:

- Does traditional instructional design work for online learning?
- How do I design with the user in mind?
- How do I make things easy to find on my site?
- How do I make sure the site is easy to navigate?

## Does Traditional Instructional Design Work for Online Learning?

When designing instructional materials, it's usually best to use a systematic approach. This is true whether you're designing a face-to-face lesson on dinosaurs, an educational video, a higher education course, or an instructional Web site. Instructional design principles, even if not followed to the exact letter, are one type of systematic approach. They represent a rigorous process for determining and meeting the needs of the intended audience.

There are many different instructional design models. Most have these things in common:

- Use of a systematic process
- Iterative stages of design, development, and evaluation
- An initial analysis stage

There are a number of philosophies for the systematic process of designing instruction, but one of the simplest to understand is the ADDIE process. This methodology was introduced by Dr. Allison Rossett in her 1987 book, *Training Needs Assessment*.

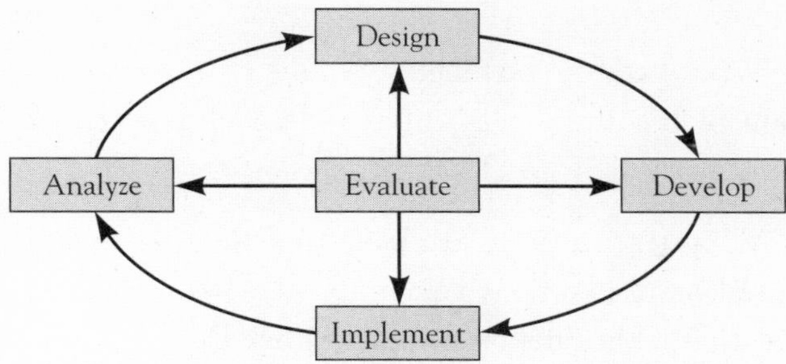


Figure 4.1. The ADDIE Model

## ADDIE Who?

ADDIE is an acronym for analysis, design, development, implementation, and evaluation. If your goal is to produce effective instructional Web sites, following a systematic process like ADDIE can help prevent you from getting off on the wrong foot, wasting resources, doing unnecessary revisions, and failing to meet the learner's needs. Figure 4.1 is a visual representation of the ADDIE model.

For those of you new to instructional design, I'll provide a quick overview of ADDIE.

### Analysis

The design of instruction, including instructional Web sites, starts with gathering information. Here are some of the primary questions we ask at this stage of design:

#### Audience

- Who is my audience?
- What do I need to know about them when developing these materials?
- What are their needs?

**Content**

- What needs to be taught?
- Which content is essential and which is nice to know?

**Resources**

- What resources are available (people, time, budget, materials, and so on)?
- What additional resources do I need?
- What organizational constraints do we have?

**Goals and evaluation criteria**

- What goals do I want to achieve?
- How will I know when I've met these goals?

### Design and Development

The two Ds in the ADDIE model, design and development, often include these activities:

**Define instructional objectives.** Objectives describe the observable performance or behavior expected of the learner. When we write objectives, we use verbs such as *select*, *demonstrate*, *list*, *recall*, *analyze*, *estimate*, *locate*, and *arrange*, but not words such as *understand*, *fully understand*, and *appreciate* (because these are neither observable nor easily measurable).

**Determine interface.**

- Determine a standardized look and feel for the site.
- Determine how the user will enter the site and get around.

**Determine instructional strategies.**

- Determine how to present information and lessons.
- Determine the content for each page.
- Determine activities and interactions.
- Determine student assessments.

**Make a flowchart or storyboard of the site.** Develop a graphic representation that shows the flow and outline of the content.

**Develop the site.** Many designers develop a prototype before creating the entire site. This allows them to test the site and gather feedback before committing additional resources.

**Produce the materials and upload to the server.**

**Collect formative evaluation data.** Gather feedback on ease of use, content, and interactions.

### Implementation

Now it's time for the I in the model: implementation. In this stage, you let the intended audience use the material and collect data to determine whether you've met your instructional objectives. If you haven't, what improvements, additions, or changes do you need to make? Do you need to do additional design and development? (This is not uncommon!)

Some instructional designers and developers implement the project on a smaller scale—for example, they test just one piece of the Web site, or they test the whole site with a small group of people. They then take what they've learned from the tests and do additional design and development to correct any problems.

### Evaluation

You've been doing some evaluation all along (for instance, the formative evaluation in the design and development phase), but now you need to analyze whether the program met the goals you set during the analysis phase. What isn't working as planned? Why? What do you need to change or add?

One of the biggest problems with traditional instructional design is that it doesn't provide guidance on selecting the most appropriate instructional activities. For that, you need to do the kind of analysis I talked about in Chapter 2. Some of us who design online instruction feel that this extra analysis should be added to the traditional model.

## Does Technology Change How We Do Instructional Design?

Technology challenges traditional assumptions about the instructional systems design (ISD) methods that trainers and instructional designers are used to. Online learning's attributes are different from those of classroom-based learning, as Table 4.1 shows.

Since the attributes are potentially different, design is likely to be different, too. Rod Simms, academic director of QANTM in Brisbane, Queensland, Australia, gives us an alternate way of looking at the design process for technology-based learning. This process takes into account the different types of people involved in the process and the types of deliverables that normally occur while designing and developing.

## Rethinking Instructional Design

Sims argues that we need to change the way we look at instructional design. In a paper published in the *Australian Journal of Educational Technology* (www.ascilite.org.au/ajet/ajet13/sims.html), he cautions that the poor courseware we're seeing today may be a result of faulty assumptions about instructional design.

Traditional instructional design is a linear, reliable, and highly sequential approach to developing instructional materials. "The problem, though, is that the prescriptive nature of this process can result in technically correct structures which spotlight content rather than interaction," Sims says. Remember how I said earlier that instructional design methods don't help you determine what activities are needed in the instruction? That's what Sims is saying here.

Table 4.1. Attributes of Classroom and Online Instruction

| Classroom Instruction | Online Instruction |
|---|---|
| Activities: Classroom | Activities: Online, field, classroom |
| Event based: Certain time and place | Process based: Potentially any time and place (24/7) |
| Interaction: Immediate | Interaction: Immediate or delayed |
| Media: Voice, print, graphics, video | Media: Web pages (text), graphics, video, audio, programming, Flash, etc. |
| Designer skills needed: Instructional design | Designer skills needed: Instructional design, graphic design, interaction design, information design, and more |
| Usability: Instructional materials are generally easy to use | Usability: Instruction can be challenging to use |
| Learner support and feedback: Immediate | Learner support and feedback: Immediate or delayed |

Sims states that technology opens up new possibilities for course design, but people often ignore those possibilities when they imitate traditional instructional techniques. I couldn't agree more.

If traditional instructional design isn't the whole answer, then what is? Perhaps some new ways of thinking can help us better harness technology to help people learn. Sims proposes that we first look at our assumptions about using technology for learning and see whether they help or hinder our efforts. Here's what Sims says about these assumptions.

*Assumption 1: Technology Makes Learning More Effective*

It's true that technology can allow us to individualize instruction and imitate reality. But instructional design models provide little guidance in doing this, which means it doesn't happen very often. And that's a problem.

*Assumption 2: Traditional Teacher-Student Interactions Must Be Maintained in Online Learning*

Should the relationship between teacher and student be the same in an online course as it is in the classroom? Lecturing, for instance, is one way instructors teach in a classroom. Does this work with technology? Not necessarily. Other instructional approaches are more appropriate for technology-delivered learning.

*Assumption 3: Online Learning Caters to Differences in Learning Styles*

Even though it's possible to develop online courses that respond to learners' individual needs, it isn't easy. Creating two or more paths through a course is more expensive, difficult, and time-consuming than creating only one. For that reason, few course developers are doing it. Sims says we need to know more about how people interact with technology before we understand how to make adaptive learning work.

*Assumption 4: Instructional Design Will Improve Course Quality*

Traditional instructional design models were designed for face-to-face instruction. Instructional design for technology-delivered learning will probably be replaced by more flexible approaches—ones that take into account what we know about how learners interact with technology.

What kinds of models might we adopt for designing technology-based learning—especially in a business environment in which it's critical to be able to rapidly respond to new learning needs?

Sims recommends a model for designing interactive instruction that I find intriguing and useful. He calls it the Interactive Instructional Influence Development Model (I3D), shown in Figure 4.2.

In this model, activities have varying amounts of influence at different times in the development of technology-based learning. The structure of the I3D model is different from traditional linear instructional design, but it uses most of the same components.

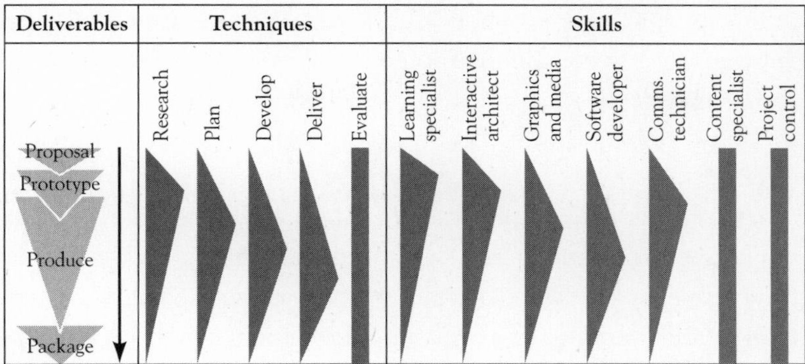


Figure 4.2. Interactive Instructional Influence Development Model (I3D)
*Source:* Sims (1997).

Here's how I3D works. Deliverables (in the left-hand column of Figure 4.2) show four steps you go through as you develop technology-based learning. The first is developing a proposal in order to get the resources you need. Next, you develop a prototype and (after getting feedback) move into development. Finally, you package the finished product for delivery to the learner.

Now move on to the Techniques column. Each of the techniques (or activities) is important throughout the project, but the peak of the triangle represents the point at which a technique is most important. In other words, the triangle shape mirrors each technique's increasing or decreasing impact during development. For instance, research is most influential at the proposal and prototyping stages but starts to decline after that. Evaluation is equally influential in each stage of the process, so it's represented by a rectangle.

The next column represents the skills you need in order to develop technology-based learning. Instructional design skills have been subdivided into those needed by the learning specialist and the interactive architect. Learning specialists use their knowledge of how people learn and how technology affects learning to select appropriate instructional strategies. Interactive architects select the best media to accomplish the tasks established by the learning specialist. (This might be the same person, but the skill sets are different.)

Again, the peak of the triangle shows where each skill is most important. For example, the skills of the learning specialist and the interactive architect are critical up front, as the project is conceptualized and designed. The software developers' skills become critical later, as they bring to life what the designers have dreamed up.

bottom line

The main point behind the I3D model is that **it doesn't make sense to force technology to replicate the face-to-face classroom. Instead, we need to see what technology allows us to do well and design toward that end.**

## How Do I Design with the User in Mind?

It's interesting to watch people using a Web site or online course you've built. When they click on the wrong button or mutter about not being able to find something, your instinct is to jump in to show them what to do. Or you may silently ridicule them for not understanding the obvious.

bottom line

But if we blame the user, we miss the point entirely. **Navigating an online course should be easy. If the user is making lots of mistakes, it's probably the designer—not the user—who's dense or misguided. That's why it's so important to focus on usability when you're designing technology-delivered instruction.**

What is usability? In his excellent book *Don't Make Me Think*, Steve Krug (2000) defines usability as "making sure that something works well: that a person of average (or even below average) ability and experience can use the thing . . . for its intended purpose without getting hopelessly frustrated."

I was talking to an instructional technology buddy about Web usability the other day, and he wondered whether the expense and time of usability testing would really pay off. "Gee, I dunno," I said. "I guess it would be better to spend umpteen dollars and a gazillion hours building a learning site, and then watch users spend hours trying to figure out how to use it—not to mention that some of them may decide not to use it at all."

To me, skipping usability testing makes about as much sense as trying to save money by building a house yourself. Instead of hiring any of those high-priced folks to help you—an architect, an electrician, a carpenter, and so forth—you go to Home Depot, pick up some supplies, and start building. And along comes the big bad wolf (or a bad hailstorm, or the county inspector) and blows your house down. The moral of this fairy tale is that what seems cheap in the short term often ends up expensive in the long term.

Perhaps I was hassling my buddy too much. It's true that return on investment (ROI) is an important concern, so if you really want numbers to justify usability efforts, check out articles on Web usability guru Jakob Nielson's Alertbox Site (http://www.useit.com/alertbox/). Usability most definitely makes cents.

### Who's the User?

The first rule of usability is "Know thy user." When I work with a client to build a learning site, I start by asking who will be using it. Many of my clients do not have a good answer to this deceptively simple question. Sure, some people can tell me the intended users' jobs, but that's usually all they know. When I try to get more detailed information about how old the users are or how much computer experience they have, I often meet resistance. "We'll build it for a generic user and others will adapt," is a common response. I tell them there's no such thing as a generic user.

bottom line

**Designing for a generic user is the same as designing for absolutely no one. It's a waste of time and resources.**

To get information about your users, start by gathering information from the people who will be using your site, including their age, gender, educational level, language, computer experience, and expectations. You can get this information by asking lots of questions of managers and users, doing user surveys, and simply watching folks work.

Another approach is to develop detailed composite models, or "personas," of potential users. For instance, one of the personas for the online courses I teach is "Madge." She's fifty-two and has been a trainer for twenty-one years. She's Internet-proficient but has her doubts about online learning. Another persona, "Tom," was a programmer before getting into instructional technology five years ago. At age thirty-eight, he enjoys the technology aspects of online learning more than the instructional aspects.

Madge and Tom aren't real people, but they represent the types of learners who take my courses. For example, I need to make sure my courses are easy to use so I don't lose Madge. At the same time, I need to build in plenty of optional technical challenges so Tom stays engaged.

bottom line

**The bottom line is that you need to know who you're designing for and who you're not designing for.** Although there is no generic user, there will likely be a group of average users—folks in the middle of the bell curve for your particular course.

### What Will They Do with It?

The next step is to figure out how your users will navigate the Web. Krug's book has a great chapter on how people use the Web, available online (http://www.sensible.com/chapter.html) (Krug, 2000). Many designers, he says, expect users to read all the text on the screen and carefully choose the most appropriate link or button. In reality, most people simply scan the page and choose the first option that's somewhat related to what they need, regardless of whether it's the best decision.

Once you know how your learners use the Web, you need to get more specific and find out how they'll use your site. Call this a user task analysis, if you will. Think about your users' location, lighting, hardware, and software. Then make adjustments. For example, if you find out that most users have poor lighting in their offices, make sure your site has a large font size and sharp contrast between colors.

You'll also want to make sure that the most important and frequent tasks are the easiest for your users to find. When I teach an online course, for example, I know the syllabus will get used a lot, so I make sure there's a link to it from every page on the site. On a learning portal, the course catalog would probably be used frequently, so why hide it three clicks from the home page? Interface designers tell us to include navigational elements (such as links and buttons) to these commonly used pages on every page. They call this "persistent navigation."

One of the most effective ways to figure out how your users will navigate your site is to give them a task such as "Find the course catalog" and ask them to think aloud while they complete the task. Take notes on what they say and how they use the site. You can even ask them to walk through your storyboards before you put up a prototype. When users describe their difficulties with your site, don't get defensive or tell them what they're doing wrong. After all, the whole point is for them to feel totally comfortable telling you what's confusing.

Figure 4.3 is a simplified example of how people use one of my courses. Because I know how users navigate and which pages they visit most often, I can design the learning site to reflect that.

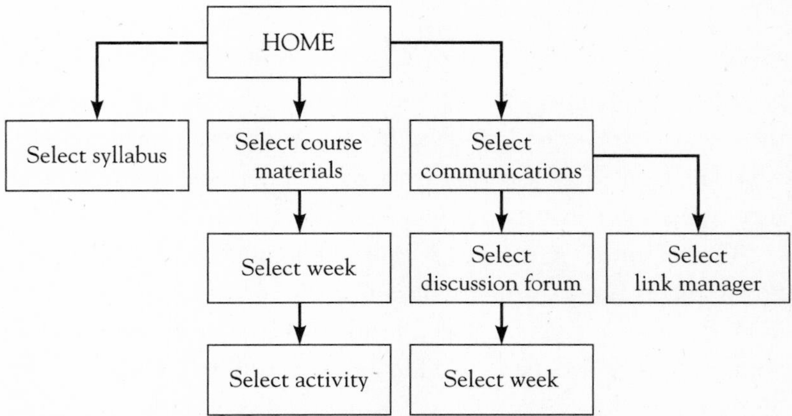


Figure 4.3. Site Design Based on Learners' Usage

Another way to find out how people use your site is to post a feedback form, asking users what worked and what didn't. Important caveat, though: It's tough to make major changes once you've already developed your site or course, so after-the-fact feedback does not substitute for gaining user information at the beginning of the design process.

### Information Underload

You hear a lot these days about information overload. But as designers, we're often working from a position of information underload: We don't have enough information about who our users are, what they need, or how they'll use the Web site.

Our work is so important and resource-intensive that we need to take every opportunity to get to know our users. After all, no engineer would design a bridge without first finding out whether it was going to be used by heavy trucks, a combination of trucks and cars, or pedestrians only.

## How Do I Make Things Easy to Find on My Site?

After you've figured out who your users are and what they'll be doing on your site, it's time to figure out how to organize the site so users can get around with minimal hassle.

### The Trouble with Categories

Let's say you're building a corporate Web site to help employees understand human resources policies. One of the hardest tasks is figuring out how to categorize the information you want to convey. Should the medical leave forms be filed under health care, regulatory compliance, family information, or policies and procedures?

The reason it's so hard to decide is that all classification systems are based on language, and language is often ambiguous. What the Web designer means by "family information" and what the user thinks it means may be very different. And how many wrong clicks will it take before the user gets frustrated and gives up?

We navigate through organizational schemes every day: phone books, the mall, television programming guides, and so forth. What makes some schemes relatively easy to figure out and others more difficult? It depends on whether the organizational scheme is exact or ambiguous.

Exact organizing schemes are easy to navigate because the information is divided into clearly delineated, mutually exclusive sections. A phone directory, for example, is divided by letters of the alphabet. If you know how to spell a person's name, you'll know exactly where to look for it. Exact organizing schemes are easy to design and maintain because there's no ambiguity in assigning items to categories.

Most Web sites, however, require ambiguous organizing schemes because the information they contain doesn't fall into precise alphabetical, chronological, or geographical delineations.

As if it isn't bad enough that language is imperfect, Web designers also have to deal with organizational politics. You know the story: Everyone wants his or her stuff to be accessible directly from the home page, making the site cluttered and indecipherable. And what about corporate sites that are organized by function—sales, finance, marketing, procurement, and so on? Those categories may make sense to the person who designed the site, but users don't necessarily know or care how the company is organized.

### Four Ways to Organize Web Content

Knowing your user (can I harp on this too much?) helps determine how you should organize your ambiguous site. Here are four of the most common ways to organize Web content.

#### *User-Organized Scheme*

A user-organized scheme can work well if you're certain the categories make sense to users. (Test to be sure; don't assume.) Here's an example of a user-organized scheme:

*XYZ Learning*

Courses for:

- Management
- IT staff
- Administrative staff

In general, users seem to have a hard time navigating within this organizational scheme. For instance, let's say I'm in the market for a new fax machine and I know exactly which brand and model I want. But when I go to the manufacturer's site, I find that it's organized by type of user: home, small business, and enterprise. Not knowing which category the fax fits into, I spend fifteen frustrating minutes searching each category. It would have been much easier for me if they had organized the site by product line.

*Organization by Topic*

Another way to organize an ambiguous site is by topic. A learning site, for example, might look like this:

*XYZ Learning*

Course types:

- Customer service
- Phone skills
- Finance
- Computer skills
- Just for fun

This is one of the hardest schemes to design correctly. The reason? Topic names mean different things to different people. Where might you find a course about dealing with angry callers, for example: under customer service or phone skills? And would a course about Quicken fall under computer skills or finance?

*Task-Organized Scheme*

Task-organized schemes are primarily used for transaction-related sites. Here's an example:

*XYZ Learning*

Online registration and bill payment:

| | |
|---|---|
| Register for courses | Change registration |
| Obtain records | Pay bill |

This type of organizational scheme works well as long as users understand what the task headings mean and the tasks correspond to how they'll use the site.

*Hybrid Scheme*

Most large sites use a hybrid of the these approaches. Consider this example:

*XYZ Learning*

About XYZ
- Stockholder information
- Student information
- Employment

Courses
- New courses
- Existing courses

Registration
- Register
- Change

The advantage of this model is that it combines the best of the other three approaches. The disadvantage is that in trying to be everything to everyone, sites like this may end up confusing people instead.

## How Do I Make Sure the Site Is Easy to Navigate?

I recently decided to buy a new iron. I went to the local Target store, looked up at the monster-sized signs, and headed over to the Small Appliances section. There were crockpots, coffee makers, toasters, electric skillets, but no irons. Frustrated, I found one of those red help-me-I'm-lost phones and asked about irons. The operator helpfully suggested I try Small Appliances. I began walking around the store, past the shoes, car parts, bath rugs, and doggie igloos. At long last, there were the irons, in the back of the store near plumbing supplies.

Despite the fact that the store had plenty of navigational elements (signs) to help me find my way, I still got lost and confused. And the backup search function (the red phone) didn't help me, either. If it weren't for my persistence, the store would have lost a $50 sale.

If you think large discount stores are hard to navigate, take a look at most Web sites. Even when visiting the most carefully designed site, you often find yourself wondering what the various icons mean and how the information is organized. Navigational elements are supposed to alleviate this frustration, but they often add to it instead.

### First, Be Conventional

When we design navigation for a Web site, we sometimes forget to think about the browser. All browsers have built-in navigational features that users know well, such as back and forward buttons, bookmarks, and the History menu.

In addition to the browser, there are other standard items that users have come to expect. For example, most visited links change colors, letting users know where they've been. And when the cursor changes from an arrow to a hand, users know they're passing over a link.

The good news is that people already know how to use these navigational features. Blue underlined text means a hyperlink, so why would a developer make these links yellow or orange or chartreuse? It's like painting a stop sign purple to match the building next to it.

Usability experts ask us to think hard before disabling or changing conventional browser features. Why not take advantage of the fact that users already understand how to operate a browser?

### Design for Different Types of Users

Users navigate Web sites and pages in different ways, depending on who they are and what they're trying to accomplish. Some are casual browsers who just want to see what's there; others have a goal and want to reach it in as few steps as possible. (In learning sites, the latter method is the more common one.) Some, when given a specific task, will try using menus, but others prefer a search function.

It's likely that you'll have all of these different types of users coming to your site, so you need to design more than one way to get from here to there. When deciding how users will navigate your site, take the following three factors into consideration:

- *Importance.* What are the most common tasks users will perform at your site? Make these tasks the most accessible.
- *Consistency.* What site elements should be on each page? Place these elements in the navigation bar, the footer (the space at the bottom of each page), or both.
- *Searchability.* Think about what types of searches your users will do. Will they look for a specific class in your course catalog, the title of a submodule in a complex course, or the next time a course will be given? The answers to these questions will help you determine whether you need a simple search engine or a more complex one.

### Navigational Models

Below are some common navigational models. Many sites combine these models into some kind of hybrid.

Hierarchical:

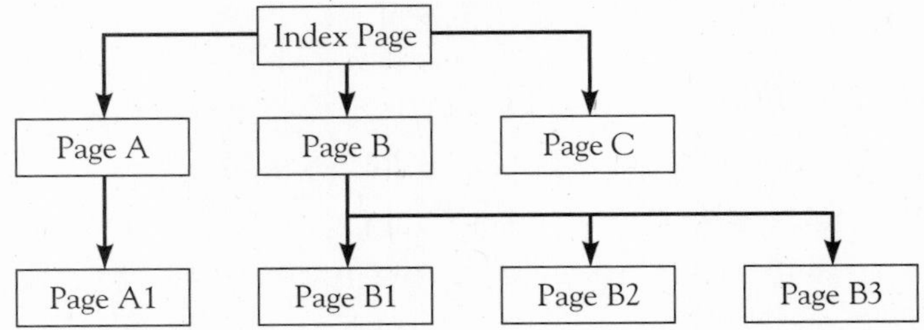


Sequential:

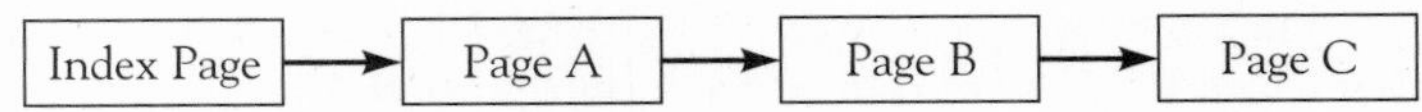


Persistent:

| Index | **Page A** |
|---|---|
| Page A | |
| Page B | |
| Page C | |

Search:

So which model makes the most sense for learning sites? Again, it depends on your users. The sequential approach is overused in training sites. That's because so many course designers are trying to model online learning after CD-ROM training or classroom instruction. Even though sequential navigation is easy for the user to follow, in most cases it's boring. Also, this approach makes it more difficult for the user to come back and find specific information. Ask yourself whether the content really has to be delivered in a lockstep manner.

Some sites truly need a sequential process—for instance, one in which users have to fill out a form to sign up for a class. But many online courses have a much less compelling need for such rigidity, since learners may need only one lesson rather than the entire course.

Hierarchical models make browsing easy and show lots of information in a relatively small amount of space. If you go to the Browse Subjects section of Amazon.com, for example, you can evaluate a wide range of books. This navigational scheme would work well for a learning site's course list.

A persistent model works best when there aren't too many levels or tasks. I've seen it used effectively for performance support (help topics listed along the left side of the screen, for instance) and for courses that are divided into modules. For example, you might see the titles of the course modules in a side column; when you click on a title, the selected module appears in the main window.

Once you've determined which navigational models work best for your site, you'll need to figure out what design elements will help users get from one place to another and back again. This could easily be the subject of an entire book, so I'll keep it short and simple for now. Here are the most common navigational elements in a Web page:

Navigation buttons and bars:

| HERE | THERE | SOMEWHERE ELSE |
|---|---|---|

Pull-down menus:

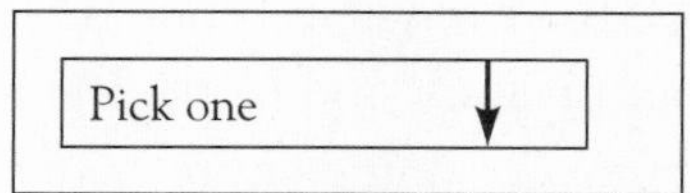


Text links: here there somewhere else

Drop-down menus:

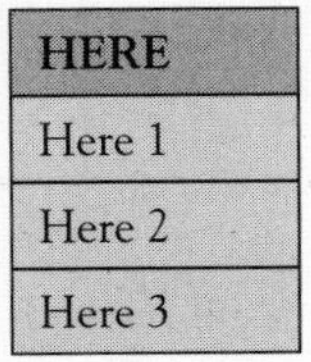


Command buttons:

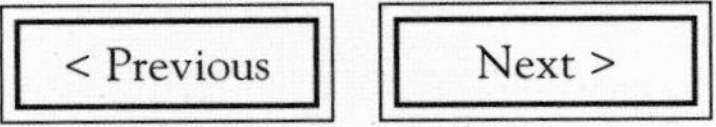


Each of these elements has its plusses and minuses. For instance, buttons clearly tell users they'll go somewhere when they click, but their titles need to stay pretty darn short. And pull-down menus conserve space but don't show the range of options until you open them.

## Conclusion

An understanding of traditional instructional design is a good jumping-off place, but you'll also need to add new steps for online learning. For one thing, there's nothing in the ADDIE model that helps you consider how to make content meaningful and engaging. Chapter 2 provides a good overview of these considerations, and I believe the model should expand to take them into account. In addition, since online learning and classroom-based learning have different attributes, we need to maximize the benefits and minimize the challenges when designing online instructional materials.

Jef Raskin sums up the importance of usability in his book *The Human Interface* (2000): "If a system's one-one-one interaction with its human user is not pleasant and facile, the resulting deficiency will poison the performance of the entire system, however fine that system might be in its other aspects."

The bottom line here is that **your success as a designer and developer of online learning is directly tied to your ability to build instructional materials that don't leave users frustrated**. To do that, make sure you gather information from learners before starting to design, go through the design process with their needs in mind, and then test the site with average users (not with client managers or corporate higher-ups) to make sure it meets their needs.

See the companion Web site for this book, http://www.learningpeaks.com/msoll/, for links to resources that will help you take the next steps to becoming more expert in this field.

# 5

# Tools and Technologies for Online Learning, Part 1

## *Development*

In the golden oldie days (about 1995 or so), a person could learn a few HTML tags, throw together some simple Web pages with clip art, and hang out a sign as a Webmaster. Those days are long gone. We've moved past the build-Web-pages-as-hobby phase, which means the learning curve for developing Web sites, instructional or otherwise, has become longer and steeper. Although this creates challenges for nontechies, our only alternative is to adapt. It's less of a hassle to learn about the technology and shape it to our needs than it is to hold it at bay—after all, why try to push a river against its current?

Yes, this technology stuff is complex, and there's a lot to learn. Does that mean those of us who design and develop instructional materials for the Web should leave it all to the techies? Not at all. You'll probably need help with complex Web sites—larger, more complicated sites are almost always developed by a team of folks with complementary skills (see Chapter 1). But in most cases, those of us who design and develop instruction can easily learn to put instructional materials on the Web.

In this chapter, I'll discuss technologies that are important for you to know about. It's not meant to be exhaustive, but it will give you an excellent start. I'll discuss the following topics:

- How do I build online learning?
- What are the most common tools used for building online instructional materials? What do I need to know to get started?
- What are some technologies I need to know about?

## How Do I Build Online Learning?

When you start thinking about building instructional materials for the Web, your first question may be, What authoring tool should I buy? That's the wrong question. The first question should be, What kinds of online learning do I need to build? (For help answering this question, see Chapter 2). Once you've figured out what you want to create, you can look for authoring tools that will help you get there.

There isn't one right authoring tool. In fact, most online learning is built with a combination of tools. Table 5.1 gives you a quick glance at some of the most popular tools and technologies for building online instructional materials. I've presented them in order of how difficult they are to master (with the least difficult first), although you may feel differently depending on what you're trying to do. For each technology, I'll describe an average learning curve for an average nontechie trainer or instructor. In the next part of the chapter, we'll describe them in more detail and show you some examples.

bottom line

So which is the right tool for you? **Take a look at the things each tool is good for and less good for, and you'll probably come to the same conclusion I have: Different tools work well for different purposes.**

Table 5.1. Tools for Building Online Instructional Materials

| | |
|---|---|
| PowerPoint | Instructors who are used to lecturing with electronic slides can put them on the Web for others to view. They can be used for overviews and presentations.<br>Tools: PowerPoint<br>Good for:<br>Providing copies of slides for review after a face-to-face presentation<br>Short narrated slide show as part of an online presentation or course<br>Less good for:<br>Full online course<br>Level of difficulty: If you know how to make PowerPoint slides, turning them into HTML-based slides is pretty easy, requiring a few simple menu commands: File>Save as Web Page. (The exact commands may vary depending on version.) |
| Text (HTML, PDF) | HTML is the programming language that formats the text on most Web pages. It has its limits, which is why other technologies have emerged to fill in the gaps. Still, HTML is the glue that holds together most Web pages, even when other technologies are used.<br>PDF, developed by Adobe, formats electronic text so that it looks exactly like the text and graphic formats from which it came (Word, PowerPoint, etc.). In order to view and print a PDF file, users must have the Adobe Acrobat Reader plug-in, which comes installed in most operating systems.<br>Tools: HTML coding by hand, Dreamweaver, Adobe Acrobat (for PDF)<br>Good for:<br>Building the foundation of almost any instructional site<br>Providing print copies of text. (Test to make sure they print well!)<br>Less good for:<br>Using alone. Since it's a foundation, HTML usually is used with other tools such as JavaScript, Flash, software simulations, streaming media, etc. |

*(continued)*

Table 5.1. Tools for Building Online Instructional Materials *(continued)*

| | |
|---|---|
| Text (HTML, PDF) *(continued)* | Level of difficulty: The basic programming tags are incredibly easy to learn. You can become proficient quickly. More complex programming tags (like tables, forms, and style sheets) are harder to learn but not impossible. |
| Asynchronous Discussion | Asynchronous discussions allow learners, instructors, and others to exchange information and ask questions, usually in text format, at different times and places.<br>Tools: E-mail, listservs, conferencing programs<br>Good for:<br>Communication among learners, instructors, facilitators, and subject-matter experts when there isn't an urgent need for real-time discussions<br>Less good for:<br>Real-time communication<br>Level of difficulty: Generally not difficult to learn for facilitating online discussion or collaboration. If the program needs to be installed on your organization's servers, your IT folks will need to help you. Some discussion programs are used on others' servers and only require that you know how to operate them. |
| Scripts | Scripts are programming languages that Web browsers or Web servers read and execute to add functionality to Web pages. They are often used for rollovers and to add interactivity.<br>Tools: JavaScript and CGI programming, Dreamweaver, CourseBuilder<br>Good for:<br>Quizzes for feedback<br>Pop-up windows<br>Interactive features (rollovers, etc.)<br>Less good for:<br>Learners who have turned JavaScript off in their browsers. They won't be able to see features you've designed in JavaScript. |

| | |
|---|---|
| Scripts *(continued)* | Level of difficulty: Not easy, but much easier if you already know HTML. Some authoring programs (like Dreamweaver) automatically write some basic scripts so you don't need to know how to write them yourself. Many people first learn how to copy and manipulate others' scripts (there are many sites just for this purpose) before learning how to write their own. |
| Animation and software simulation | Animations are ideal for showing changes and processes. They're also great for simulations, which allow users to interact with software in a controlled environment.<br>Tools: Flash, ViewletBuilder, RoboDemo, RapidBuilder<br>Good for:<br>Showing structure, sequence, process<br>Demonstrating concepts<br>Allowing learners to interact in a simulated environment<br>Less good for:<br>Very low-bandwidth situations, although the file sizes for the finished products are often reasonably small<br>Level of difficulty: Flash has a pretty steep learning curve, if you want to do anything creative with it. Simple software simulation programs (RoboDemo, ViewletBuilder) are easier to learn. |
| Databases and middleware | Databases, when used with Web sites, allow users to customize a page through their input. For example, a user might tell the database to sort items by date or name.<br>Middleware communicates with a database and returns the results so a browser can read them.<br>Middleware tools: ColdFusion, ASP and PHP programming<br>Databases: MySQL, Oracle, Access |

*(continued)*

Table 5.1. Tools for Building Online Instructional Materials *(continued)*

| | |
|---|---|
| Databases and middleware *(continued)* | Good for:<br>Content that needs to change according to learner needs<br>Less good for:<br>Simple sites or just-getting-started situations. This is complex stuff, and you won't be able to use it if you don't have knowledge about or access to the technologies.<br>Level of difficulty: Developing pages that pull content from a database requires advanced skills. Save this for the future or get help from experienced developers. |
| Streaming media | Streaming media formats allow audio and video to be delivered to the user quickly, without being downloaded to the user's hard drive.<br>Tools: QuickTime, Real Producer, Windows MediaPlayer<br>Good for:<br>Content showing real action<br>Less good for:<br>"Talking heads"<br>Low-bandwidth situations<br>Level of difficulty: Producing streaming media requires a wide range of skills: production, editing, development, and more. Save this for the future or get help from experienced developers. |

## What Are the Most Common Tools Used for Building Online Instructional Materials? What Do I Need to Know to Get Started?

The following tools, used separately or together, will help you design and build online instructional materials.

### PowerPoint

Putting your PowerPoint slides on the Web is easy. Within PowerPoint, simply select Save as Web Page from the file menu. That's why so many folks do it. But the file sizes are generally quite large, and long, online PowerPoint presentations (especially if there isn't any interactivity) are dreadfully boring.

In some cases, converting PowerPoint slides directly into Web content makes sense. Let's say you attended my in-person presentation and wanted copies of my slides. I could save them as Web pages and upload them for you to review. (See Figure 5.1.) The menu on the left, which is automatically generated by PowerPoint when you save the presentation as a Web page, allows users to navigate easily through the slides.

There are some new tools—Macromedia's Breeze and eHelp's RoboPresenter, for instance—that let you record narration to go with your slides and save the final output as Flash. This is much better than just uploading a bunch of slides. I recently attended an online conference on learning objects (www.nmc.org) using Breeze. It was a terrific experience.

### HTML

The Web started as a place to share simple documents. Hypertext Markup Language (HTML), a *very* simple coding language, was developed to handle the task. Because it was so easy to use, lots of people learned it and the Web grew quickly. But HTML's simplicity quickly became a problem for folks who wanted to put more complex materials on the Web.

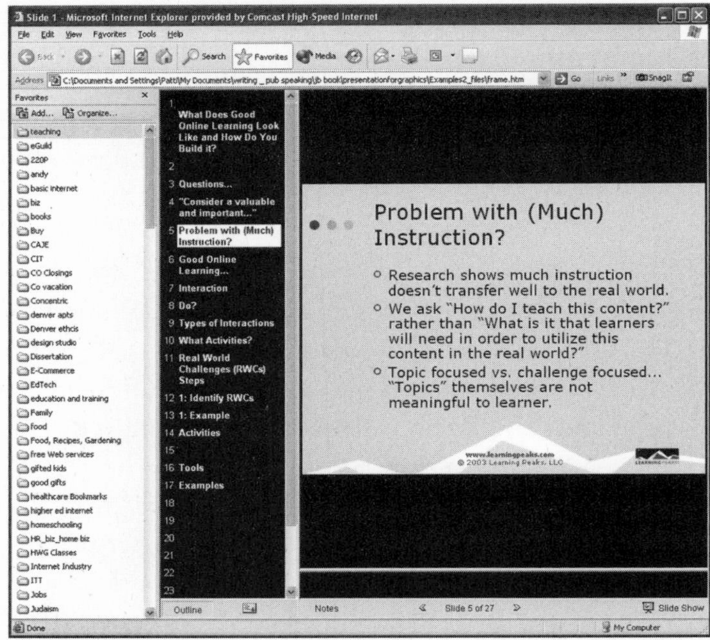


Figure 5.1. My Presentation on Interaction Saved as HTML Pages

HTML tells a computer how to display and format the items on a Web page. HTML documents are text files coded with "tags" that tell a Web browser how to format that text. Let's say I want this text to show up on a Web page:

**Hi!** My name is *Eric*.

Here's the HTML you would write to tell the browser to show the first word as bold and the last word as italic:

<b>Hi!</b>My name is <i>Eric.</i>

The <b></b> tags tell the browser to start and stop bold. The <i> and </i> tell the browser to start and stop italic. It's that easy!

Authoring tools such as Dreamweaver make producing HTML pages easier by generating the code for you. Using the example

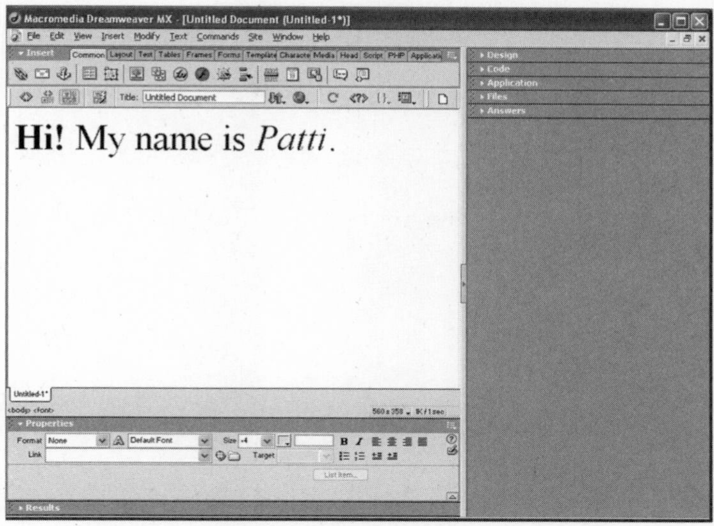


Figure 5.2. Dreamweaver's Design View Window

above, you would type in "Hi!" and then click on the Bold button, just like you do in your everyday word-processing software. Dreamweaver would then automatically add the HTML code to set the word in boldface type. Because of that, Dreamweaver is what we call a WYSIWYG editor. WYSIWYG (pronounced *wizzy-wig*) stands for "what you see is what you get." In other words, you see the word "Hi" in bold, and that's exactly what you get.

Let's take a look at Figure 5.2. In Dreamweaver's WYSIWYG window (called Design View), you type in the text and use the properties inspector (look below the big white editing window) to change text to bold and italic.

Where's the HTML? Click on the HTML icon at the top to open the HTML editing window (in Dreamweaver, this is called Code View). See Figure 5.3 (next page).

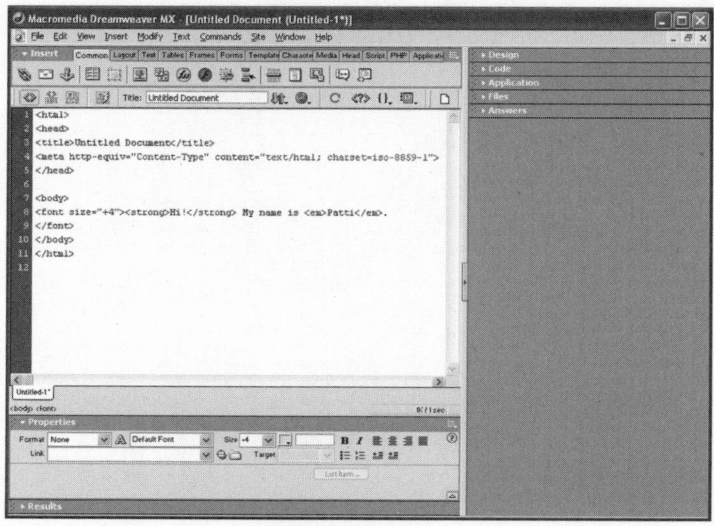


Figure 5.3. Dreamweaver's Code View Window

At the same time I'm using the WYSIWYG window to create my page, the HTML is being produced automatically in the background. If you know HTML and want to revise the actual code, you can open the HTML window (by clicking on the icon) and change the code right there. Then when you close the HTML window, the WYSIWYG window shows the changes you made. Going back and forth between the two views is known in Dreamweaver speak as "roundtrip HTML."

## JavaScript

JavaScript is a programming language that adds dynamic elements to Web pages. In other words, it creates Web pages that don't just sit there; they *do* something. This language works in JavaScript-enabled browsers, which includes all major 4.x-plus browsers. Some JavaScript code runs slightly differently on different browsers.

How does JavaScript code make a Web page do something? Through objects, properties, methods, and event handlers. Now don't let your eyes glaze over—this is really pretty simple.

Let's start with *objects*. In the real world, objects are things like chairs, potato chip bags, and light bulbs. In the Web world, the page itself is an object and so are the things on the page: tables, links, forms, images, and buttons. Each of these objects has certain *properties*. Just as a chair can be green or blue, Web pages can have different background colors. Here's how a yellow background color would look in JavaScript code:

```
document.bgcolor="yellow"
```

The object is the Web page (called "document" in JavaScript) and the property is the background color (bgcolor). The bgcolor property in the example is set to equal yellow.

Most objects can do certain things. These things are called *methods*. A light bulb (object) can be turned on and off (methods). A potato chip bag (object) can be opened or crumpled up (methods). A Web page (object) can be opened or closed (methods). Here's how that would look in JavaScript code:

```
document.open()
document.close()
```

*Event handlers* cause changes when certain things occur. Think of it this way: If you drop something fragile, it can shatter. What's the event that caused the shattering? Dropping it. Here's a Web page example: When you roll your mouse over a link, a message pops up in the browser status bar (the gray bar at the bottom of the browser). In this example, the JavaScript event handler is called onMouseOver. It loads the desired message into the status bar.

Here's what the JavaScript code might look like if you wanted the phrase "Hey, whatcha doing?" to appear in the status bar as your mouse runs over a link that says, "Put mouse here."

```
<A HREF=""onMouseOver="window.status=
'Hey, whatcha doing?';
return true;">Put mouse here.</A>
```

You may be wondering whether you have to learn JavaScript code to use it in your instructional Web pages. The answer is no, but it's likely that you will eventually want to learn something about it. There are plenty of free and inexpensive scripts that you can cut and paste into your HTML code. And Dreamweaver, my favorite Web authoring tool, will code some of it for you.

We've already talked about a few things JavaScript can do. It can also

- Update the date at the top of the Web page
- Provide feedback on a simple quiz
- Change an image when you perform a certain action (for instance, clicking on a button)
- Show a pop-up window when the user clicks on a button

Figure 5.4 is an example of a pop-up window being developed inside Dreamweaver.

And Figure 5.5 shows what it looks like in a browser window on page 87.

Figures 5.6 and 5.7 on page 88 provide examples from a real instructional site I built. It uses JavaScript-based CourseBuilder (a free Dreamweaver quiz-building add-on) to provide feedback on some online cases.

### Flash

I've always liked Flash. Its plug-in is included in most operating systems and browsers, so the installed user base is huge. Flash uses vector-based animation, which usually creates extremely small file sizes. These small files stream (play while downloading) easily, even

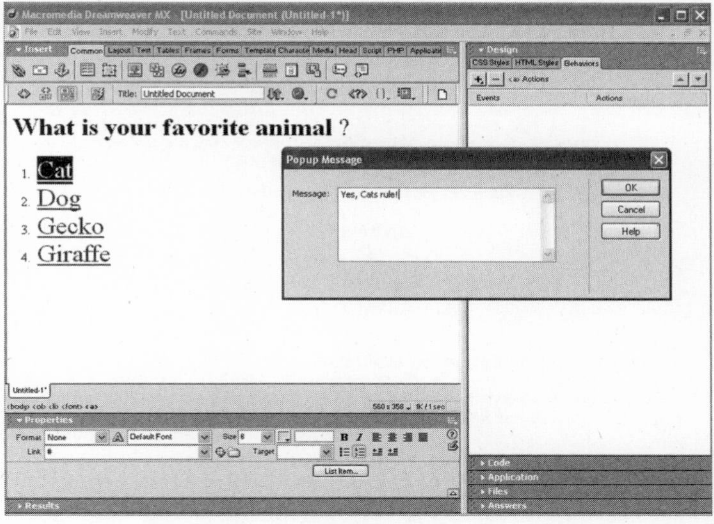


Figure 5.4. Pop-up Window in Dreamweaver

**What is your favorite animal** ?

1. Cat
2. Dog
3. Gecko
4. Giraffe

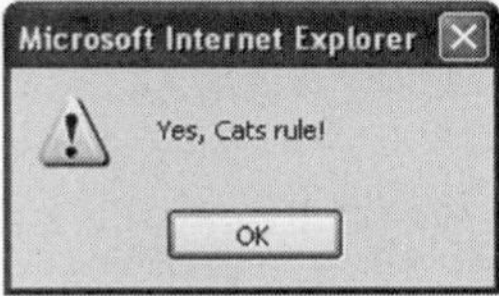


Figure 5.5. Pop-up Window in Browser

at low bandwidth. Flash also integrates easily into standard Web authoring packages such as Dreamweaver.

Flash isn't the easiest application to learn, but it's not out of reach for instructional designers and developers. Developing decent Flash learning content simply requires some study and practice.

If you've seen nothing more of Flash content than those mind-numbing eye-candy splash screens, you may be shaking your head

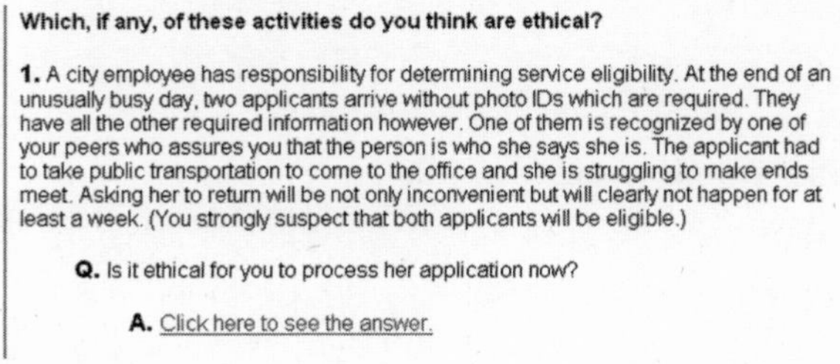

**Which, if any, of these activities do you think are ethical?**

**1.** A city employee has responsibility for determining service eligibility. At the end of an unusually busy day, two applicants arrive without photo IDs which are required. They have all the other required information however. One of them is recognized by one of your peers who assures you that the person is who she says she is. The applicant had to take public transportation to come to the office and she is struggling to make ends meet. Asking her to return will be not only inconvenient but will clearly not happen for at least a week. (You strongly suspect that both applicants will be eligible.)

**Q.** Is it ethical for you to process her application now?

**A.** Click here to see the answer.

Figure 5.6. Prompt

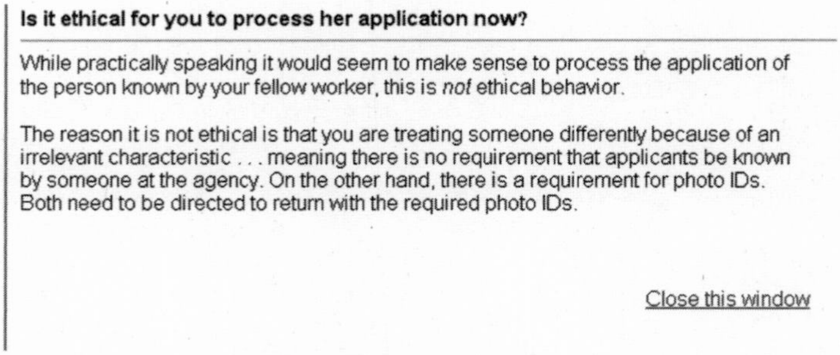

**Is it ethical for you to process her application now?**

While practically speaking it would seem to make sense to process the application of the person known by your fellow worker, this is *not* ethical behavior.

The reason it is not ethical is that you are treating someone differently because of an irrelevant characteristic . . . meaning there is no requirement that applicants be known by someone at the agency. On the other hand, there is a requirement for photo IDs. Both need to be directed to return with the required photo IDs.

Close this window

Figure 5.7. Answer

in disgust and wondering where my good sense has gone. It's true that there's loads of Flash eye candy littering the Internet. But whose fault is that? Not the tool's, for heaven's sake. People can and will use any tool to produce meaningless content.

Some tools create painful problems, such as platform and browser incompatibilities and screen resolution issues. If you have total control over all these issues (for example, your course will be delivered over a corporate intranet using one platform, one browser, and consistent screen resolution), this isn't a big deal. But if you're developing for a wide Internet-based audience, these incompatibilities can make you want to tear out your hair—and the hair of everyone around you.

Flash doesn't have these problems. If users have the Flash plug-in, they see exactly what you've developed, regardless of platform, browser type, and screen resolution. This is a huge plus.

bottom line

**In instructional sites, Flash works best for any instruction that shows motion, structure, or sequence.** For example, imagine an online orientation that allows learners to walk through the floor plan of a building. Or a product demo that lets a salesperson view a virtual demo of a new laser copier and click on parts of it for explanations.

Because Flash seems to be commonly misunderstood, let's take a look at some examples so you'll have a feel for what it can really do. These examples are just a small sampling of what's possible. And remember, it's hard to depict animation in print, so make sure you look at live examples on the Web. Start with Macromedia's showcase of instructionally oriented materials: http://dynamic.macromedia.com/bin/MM/showcase/scripts/showcase_cs_listing_by_query.jsp?industry=Education/Training.

Teaching Matters is a Flash animation that shows how technology can be integrated into scientific inquiry. Its purpose is to drive in-person and online discussions among teachers. As users click on the numbers, they are shown how technology can be integrated into the activity. (See Figure 5.8 on the next page.)

The Departments of Spanish and Portuguese, Speech Pathology and Audiology, and Academic Technologies at the University of Iowa have produced some amazing animated libraries of the phonetic sounds of Spanish and English. For every consonant and vowel, there is an animated diagram, a description, and video-audio of the sound spoken in context. The site is intended for students of phonetics, linguistics, and foreign language. (See Figure 5.9 on the next page.)

Figure 5.10 (page 91) is an example of a Flash drag-and-drop exercise built for a course on Western religions at Mount Royal College in Calgary, Alberta.

When teaching complex concepts to medical students, it helps to be able to show structure and sequence—something that's hard

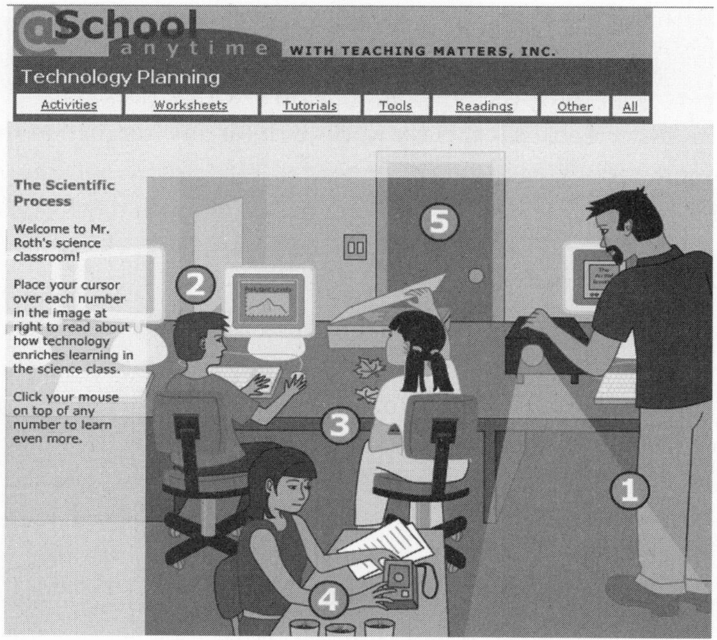


Figure 5.8. The Scientific Process, Teaching Matters
*Source:* www.atschool.org/materials/principals/planning/index.htm

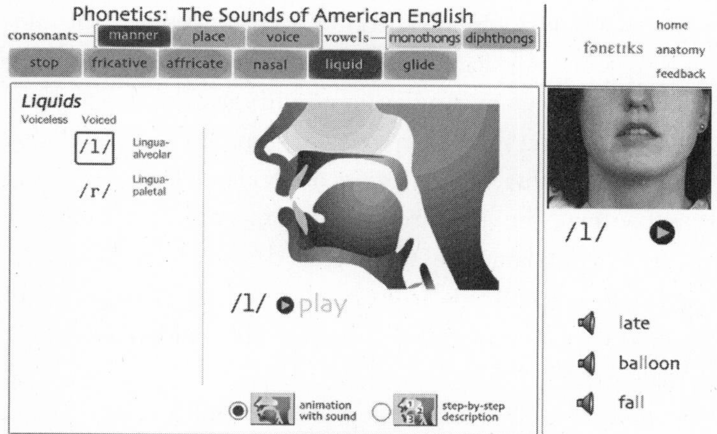


Figure 5.9. Phoneticks Flash Animation Project
*Source:* www.uiowa.edu/~acadtech/phonetics/

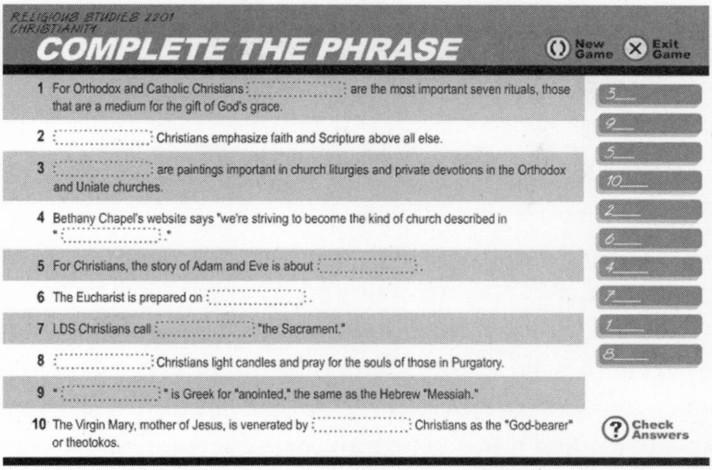

RELIGIOUS STUDIES 2201
CHRISTIANITY

COMPLETE THE PHRASE

New Game | Exit Game

1 For Orthodox and Catholic Christians __________ are the most important seven rituals, those that are a medium for the gift of God's grace.

2 __________ Christians emphasize faith and Scripture above all else.

3 __________ are paintings important in church liturgies and private devotions in the Orthodox and Uniate churches.

4 Bethany Chapel's website says "we're striving to become the kind of church described in "__________."

5 For Christians, the story of Adam and Eve is about __________.

6 The Eucharist is prepared on __________.

7 LDS Christians call __________ "the Sacrament."

8 __________ Christians light candles and pray for the souls of those in Purgatory.

9 "__________" is Greek for "anointed," the same as the Hebrew "Messiah."

10 The Virgin Mary, mother of Jesus, is venerated by __________ Christians as the "God-bearer" or theotokos.

3__
9__
5__
10__
2__
6__
4__
7__
1__
8__

Check Answers

Figure 5.10. Christianity Learning Activity

*Source:* http://www.acad-prep.mtroyal.ab.ca/adc/rels2201/activities/activities_demo.htm

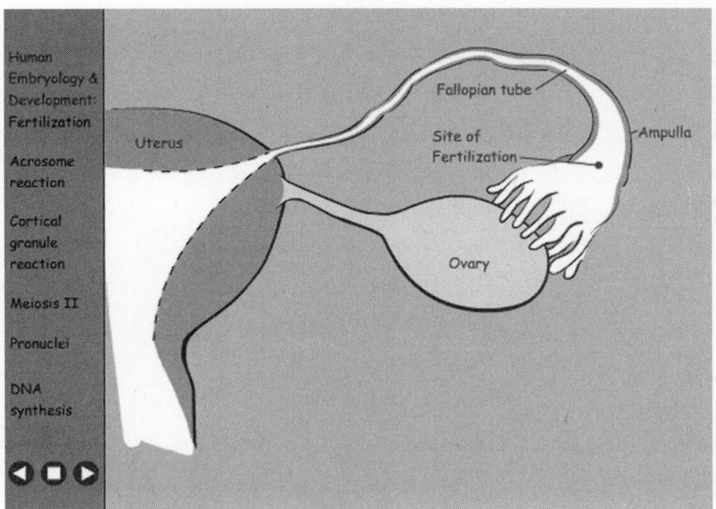


Figure 5.11. Fertilization

*Source:* PS-http://www.helenmacfarlane.com (click on animation and then Fertilization)

to do in print. Medical illustrator Helen Macfarlane produced a Flash animation showing the process of fertilization for the University of Colorado Health Sciences Center. (See Figure 5.11.)

### Software Simulations

When I ask my clients and students what kinds of learning content they want to put online, a common answer is application or software instruction. That's not surprising, as more than half the online learning out there is related to information technology. Almost all organizations need to provide training for software or proprietary applications, and the Web can be an efficient way to do this. One common method is to add text instructions to a static screen shot: "Click on the pfttt button in the navigation bar to get to the bleeblah screen." This isn't awful, but it's not engaging, either.

Figure 5.12 shows an example of using screenshots to teach one of Dreamweaver's site features. Even though the user cannot interact with these static images (a minus), this tutorial can be used as a performance support tool to help users remember how to upload files to the Web.

Some folks use live application sharing (software such as WebEx or NetMeeting) for this purpose. But this means a live person must be available at a specific time to train users on the software, which isn't possible in all situations. Asynchronous, help-on-demand solutions often make more sense.

### Two Types of Simulation Tools

If you want to create just-like-the-real-thing software simulations, there are several high-end tools to help you do it. These simulations duplicate every menu and function of the real software so people feel as though they're using the actual application. Some of the products in this category are Global Knowledge's OnDemand (http://kp.globalknowledge.com), X.HLP's X.HLP Designer (www.xhlp-usa.com), and XStream Software's RapidBuilder (http://

**Step 4 - Connect and copy your files**

**Step 4a - Connect to the remote computer**

After you tell Dreamweaver about your local computer and about the remote computer, Dreamweaver displays the contents of your Local Folder on the right side of the Site window.

Click the **Connect** button to connect to the ouray web server.

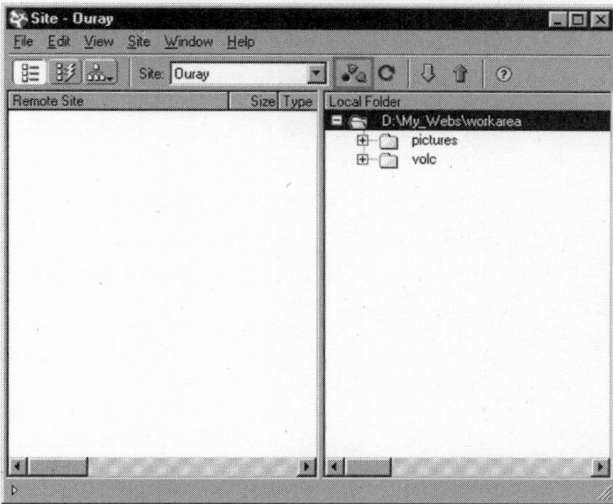


Figure 5.12. Screenshot-Based Tutorial on Connecting to Server by Using Dreamweaver

www.xstreamsoftware.com/). These products are expensive and the learning curve for developing full-featured simulations is quite steep. Still, if you truly need to duplicate all the functionality of an application, these tools fit the bill.

Let's say, though, that you want to reduce help desk calls by providing quick tutorials for users' most frequently asked questions. Or perhaps you've updated a software application and need to show users what's changed since the last version. You don't need a full-blown, just-like-the-real-thing simulation, but you may need more than just screen shots.

There are a number of inexpensive and easy-to-learn tools that make it simple to produce software demos and interactive simulations. I've tried the ones in Table 5.2 and like them all.

Table 5.2. Tools to Produce Software Demos and Simulations

| Tool | URL and Price |
|---|---|
| TechSmith's Camtasia Studio | http://www.camtasia.com/products/studio/default.asp<br>$249 at press time |
| Qarbon's ViewletBuilder | http://www.qarbon.com/products/viewletbuilder/<br>Free to $899 at press time |
| eHelp's RoboDemo | http://www.ehelp.com/products/robodemo/<br>$399 at press time |

Camtasia (by the folks who produce SnagIt, my favorite screen capture program) allows you to shoot videos of the activity on your screen, then produces demo videos of that activity. There's not a lot of interactivity, but it's much better than screen shots. ViewletBuilder allows you to add some interactivity to the demos. RoboDemo incorporates reasonably robust interactions (click spots, feedback and scoring, and so on) into your simulations.

Figure 5.13 shows a screen from a simple tutorial I built using RoboDemo. The goal is to teach users how to move files from their hard drive to the Web. The learner interacts with the tutorial by clicking on certain areas and typing in information.

**Databases**

You may have noticed that commercial Web sites are becoming more and more sophisticated. Amazon.com welcomes you back by name and bases its book suggestions on titles you've purchased

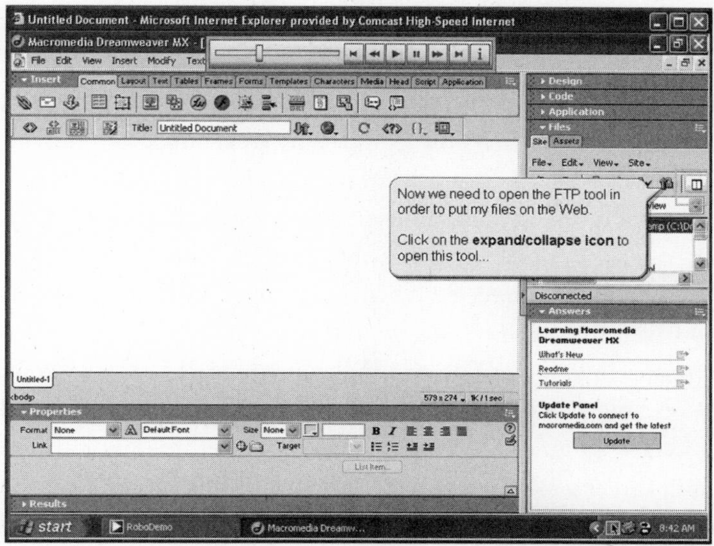


Figure 5.13. RoboDemo Tutorial for Putting Files on the Web

before. Travel sites know your originating airport the minute you log in, based on previous flights you've booked.

They do it by putting a teeny information file called a "cookie" on your hard drive. The cookie tells the site who you are and what you did during your last visit. The site then compares that information with an online database of the company's products and services, hoping to provide you with personalized suggestions that will entice you to lay down more of your hard-earned cash. It's ingenious. And it works.

How do Web pages and online databases talk to each other? They do it through something called *middleware*. Middleware connects Web pages and online databases, allowing a Web browser to access certain data from the database. The middleware product communicates with the database product and returns the results in HTML so a browser can read them.

Here's a simplified explanation of how it works. After the user selects some criteria from forms on a Web page, the middleware product takes that "query" to a database, gets the information the user has requested (houses in a certain price range, for example, or current auctions for an autographed hockey stick on eBay), and returns the information as a dynamic (built-to-order) Web page.

What does this have to do with learning? In my opinion, database-driven instructional sites will become much more common in the future. Imagine a Web site that remembers what you struggled with on your last visit and suggests some remediation tailored to your needs. Or an online catalog of course offerings tailored to your job and career goals. Or even an online new-hire orientation course that automatically displays the most recent photos and audio clips of top execs, sidestepping the need to redevelop the course each time an executive comes or goes.

### Streaming

If you have audio or video files you want folks to see on the Web, you'll probably need to use streaming techniques. Streaming allows these humongous files to start playing as they're being downloaded; that way, the user doesn't have to download the entire file first. To view streaming audio or video, users need media player plug-ins. The most common are Real Player, QuickTime, and Windows Media Player.

## What Are Some Technologies I Need to Know About?

Let's move away from specific tools for building online learning, and talk about some technologies you ought to know something about. Some of these technologies will have a big impact on learning sites now and in the future.

## Open-Source Software

Open-source software has a license that specifies that the software's source code is freely available. Contrast this with, for example, word processing software. The word processor has a license that allows a single copy of the "compiled" source code product to be used. It does not allow the user access to the source code (say, to fix bugs or add features) and it does not allow anyone to make additional copies.

The word "open" means the software is free of charge, but there is no restriction on selling the software to people who are willing to pay for convenience. That's why Red Hat (Linux) makes money selling its open-source software on CD-ROMs. Users find it easier to pay for the CD than to download hundreds of megabytes.

Most proprietary software (your word processing and spreadsheet programs, for example) comes in a binary executable format. When you click on an icon that has an .exe extension, the program gets loaded but you never see the actual code. That's because the code is proprietary, and its creators don't want you to see it or modify it.

On the other hand, open-source files that are available for people to read are stored in a text format, even though the text may look like gobbledygook to a nonprogrammer. The source code for a Web page, for example, is a text file. That means a person can read it and modify it. To be labeled "open source," software must meet certain criteria and be certified by the Open Source Initiative (www.opensource.org).

There are several types of open-source software. The best known is Linux, an open-source version of UNIX. Many well-known organizations are using it or are building software to run on it. A host of big players are endorsing Linux as a platform for their software, including IBM, Hewlett-Packard, Oracle, and Apple.

Although Linux gets the most ink, there's open-source software for just about anything you can think of, including Apache, Netscape (Mozilla), and mySQL.

What does this have to do with learning? Lots, potentially. Open-source software is used extensively in computer science curricula because access to the source code makes it a wonderful teaching tool. It's used less in other disciplines simply because teachers don't know enough about it. There are a number of educational products built on open-source programming languages, though, and certainly more will follow.

## XML

XML, or eXtensible Markup Language, makes it easier to translate data from one type of document into another. In other words, XML enables heterogeneous systems to exchange data homogeneously. It was developed by the World Wide Web Consortium (www.w3.org), a standards organization whose goal is to make sure the Web stays interoperable.

First, a few definitions. The word "extensible" (the X in XML) refers to the ability to extend capabilities. Specifically, this means XML is able to add new markup tags on the fly. Markup tags are the symbols in a text file that explain how the file should look when it's printed or shown on screen, or how it's structured. You'll usually hear these symbols called "tags." For example, this paragraph is indented; therefore, the document's markup has to explain to the printer (or screen) to indent the first line.

Since HTML and XML are both markup languages, they have some similarities. For instance, they both use tags with angle brackets (the <> around the tag).

A primary difference between HTML and XML is how you use them. HTML tags primarily describe how the text should be *presented*. Here's an example of HTML:

```
<h3>Bancroft PS3523.O46 A6 1993</h3>
<b>The science fiction stories of Jack London</b>
```

```
<br>London, Jack
<br>Carol Publishing group
```

The output of these HTML tags looks like this:

Bancroft PS3523.O46 A6 1993

**The science fiction stories of Jack London**

London, Jack

Carol Publishing group

Although the HTML code tells us how to display the text, it doesn't tell us anything about what the content is. This might not be important for a single, isolated Web page, but it becomes much more critical if we're trying to use that content in a variety of places.

If XML were used to mark up the same text as above, it might look like this:

```
<book>
<call_number>Bancroft PS3523.O46 A6 1993</call_number>
<title>The science fiction stories of Jack London</title>
<author>London, Jack</author>
<publisher>Carol Publishing group</publisher>
</book>
```

XML makes it possible to share this information among various systems. So the information about Jack London, for example, could be used in a print-based catalog, an online bookstore, and a fiction authors' database. **HTML describes how the data looks, whereas XML describes what the data is.**

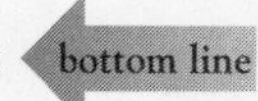


*Understanding XML*

Here's an example to help you understand extensible markup. Like most people, I make a list before I go grocery shopping. On my list, I group items by aisle or section—for example, things like skim milk and cheddar cheese tend to be in the same part of the store, as do tomato soup and applesauce. I organize the list myself, but wouldn't it be nice if technology could help do it for me? Let's say, in order to more easily sort my list, I create sorting categories (that is, markup) like this:

Dairy: skim milk

Canned: tomato soup

Dairy: cheddar cheese

Canned: applesauce

A list-sorting program would look something like this:

```
if(item starts with "Canned:")
then move item toward end of list
if(item starts with "Dairy:")
then move item toward beginning of list
```

So now I can put my list through the list-sorting program and voilà! My list gets sorted so all the dairy products are together and all the canned stuff is together.

Now let's take a look at what the non-XML world of data is like. Let's say I get sick and my neighbor offers to do my shopping for me. My neighbor, in an attempt to save time by merging her list with mine, tries to put my list through her list-sorting application. It doesn't work, because her program uses different sorting categories (that is, markup) for these same items:

Wet_dairy->skim milk

Can->tomato soup

Dry_dairy->cheddar cheese

Can->applesauce

We use the same data (skim milk, tomato soup, cheddar cheese, applesauce), but our data isn't formatted (marked up) the same way. Our applications can't use each other's data unless we have a utility to convert from one format to another. Such a utility, if it existed, would need to know that the first dairy item on my list, "Dairy: skim milk," should become "Wet_dairy->skim milk" and the second dairy item, "Dairy: cheddar cheese," should become "Dry_dairy->cheddar cheese."

And here's another problem. Let's say I adopt a baby and add "Infant: diapers" to my shopping list. The list-sorting program doesn't have a clue what "Infant:" means. So my program either becomes less useful as I come up with new grocery categories, or I have to add more code to handle the "Infant" tag.

How might an extensible markup language help? Let's go back to the grocery lists. In XML, my categories and my neighbor's are both formatted the same way, with the <> brackets.

*My List*

```
<dairy>skim milk</dairy>
<canned>tomato soup</canned>
<dairy>cheddar cheese</dairy>
<canned>applesauce</canned>
```

*My Neighbor's List*

```
<wet_dairy>skim milk</wet_dairy>
<can>tomato soup</can>
<dry_dairy>cheddar cheese</dry_dairy>
<can>applesauce</can>
```

You're probably thinking that the tags are still different. Ah, yes, the tags are still different, but the structure of the markup (<tag>

and </tag>) is the same. Because the tags have identical structures, it's much simpler to translate the data.

XML has built-in standards that describe how to translate from one kind of tag to another. This technology can easily translate from <canned> to <can> and from </wet_dairy> to <dairy>.

And since XML is extensible, new tags can be added as needed. So if I need to add <infant>formula</infant> it's not a big deal at all.

*XML and Online Learning*

How does the shopping example apply to online learning? Let's say you write markup code for a multiple-choice quiz like this:

Choice 1: correct

Choice 2: incorrect

Choice 3: incorrect

Choice 4: correct

And someone else does it this way:

C1->right

C2->wrong

C3->wrong

C4->right

A non-XML learning management system (LMS) written to understand the first set of markup tags wouldn't understand the second set of tags, which were written for a different LMS. And just as in the diaper example earlier, if the markup included only multiple-choice questions, you'd run into problems if you decided to include fill-in-the-blank interactions later.

You've no doubt heard the buzz surrounding interoperability, learning objects, standards, and metadata; they all relate to an effort to make design and development more efficient and the results (the learning itself) better. **If we want to build content that works here**

bottom line

**and there, content has to play nicely in a variety of systems (in**

**other words, it has to be interoperable). That means all the systems have to understand the same data.** And since sharing data is a huge concern in other industries besides online learning, the solution is likely to be XML.

Who else thinks so? If you look at the information on the Advanced Distributed Learning site (www.adlnet.org), you'll see that XML is widely viewed as an important part of online learning's future. In a training session I recently helped facilitate for federal government training directors, two of the technically oriented presenters talked about XML. It's on their radar screen, so it's a good idea for us to put it on ours. Planning for our future makes our jobs extensible, too.

## Conclusion

As I mentioned at the beginning of this chapter, this can seem like pretty complicated stuff. The best way to get started is to dig in and learn something. I think it makes sense to start with HTML and then learn a basic all-around authoring tool like Dreamweaver. Because we're talking about ever-evolving technology, be prepared to evolve and learn.

The good news is that once you start learning, it gets easier and easier to learn more. In the authoring training I do with clients and students, most folks are pleased at how quickly they reach a basic level of proficiency. In a three-day workshop I facilitated at an industry conference, for instance, many of the participants were surprised to gain basic skills quickly and not too painfully. I remember one in particular who walked in the first morning totally intimidated and left saying, "Wow, this isn't so hard!" It truly isn't rocket science.

See the companion Web site for this book, http://www.learningpeaks.com/msoll/, for links to resources that will help you take the next steps to becoming more expert in this field.

6

# Tools and Technologies for Online Learning, Part 2

## *Infrastructure*

The process of getting online instructional materials from concept to implementation has many steps. In Chapters 2 and 4 we discussed the needs of learners and the design of online learning. In Chapter 5, we discussed how you can use authoring tools and programming to help your designs become instructional materials. Once you've developed these instructional materials, of course, you need to get them to the right learners at the right time. This chapter describes some of the ways you can use technology to make that happen.

In this chapter, we will address the following questions:

- What is learning infrastructure?
- What tools can I use to track learners and courses?
- What tools can I use to keep track of online content?
- What are learning objects, and how do they relate to tracking and managing online content?
- What are learning standards?

## What Is Learning Infrastructure?

When classroom-based learning was the only type of instruction available, keeping track of learners and classes was the job of a training administrator. This person manually recorded courses and registrations, kept track of which people needed certain courses, and sent out reminders when those courses became available. The training administrator logged completion of courses and provided reports to managers and administrators. For instance, he may have been asked to send periodic reports to managers with information about who hadn't completed yearly regulatory training and which people were eligible for the next course in a series. Often, this person also tracked what equipment needed to be set up in which classroom and which trainers were available at certain times.

In many organizations, especially small to mid-size ones, online and classroom-based instruction is still tracked manually. But like many manual tasks that have since become automated, these tasks can now be managed by software.

bottom line

What we're talking about here is infrastructure to support courses, designers, developers, administrators, and learners. **Not everyone is using these technologies, but it's a good idea to know about them no matter what—they may affect you in ways you haven't anticipated.** If you work for a small organization with few learners and courses, your organization may not need complex technologies to manage your learners and courses (but it may in the future). If your organization is larger, there's a good chance you've already purchased them or are considering it.

The following strategists in Sun Microsystems Learning Systems Innovations group in Broomfield, Colorado, provided me with some of the information for this chapter: Chuck Ferguson, Sandra Elvington, and Caron Newman.

## What Tools Can I Use to Track Learners and Courses?

If you're like others who are considering developing online instructional materials, chances are that you have learners scattered across various locations, maybe even all over the globe. You want to make it easy for them to access your materials on your company's network or on the Internet. You probably also want to make it easy for them to register for courses and track their progress—and you want to make your own life easier by automatically tracking which materials learners use and how they score on assessments.

You've probably heard the acronym LMS tossed around at trade shows and in industry magazines and newsletters. LMS stands for learning management system, and although its inner workings can be very complicated, its mission is simple: to automate administrative tasks such as creating course catalogs, registering users, tracking which courses users take, recording data about learners, and providing reports to managers.

These tasks sound familiar, right? They're the same tasks that the training administrator used to do manually. But instead of having Linda Learner call Joe Training Administrator to sign up for the series of online certification courses, she can do it online. Joe can see at a glance which courses have a long waiting list and schedule more sessions of that class, if necessary. And when Marty, Linda's boss, wants to know whether Linda is completing the classes according to a planned schedule, he can log into the system and find out without having to track Joe down.

Although an LMS is a computerized system, it doesn't have to track only online learning. Some LMSs also track various aspects of classroom-based learning, including which equipment (projectors, screens, and so forth) is available in which classroom and which instructors can teach certain classes.

For the most part, an LMS focuses on tracking learners. It conveys which employees fit into certain job categories (sales engineers or middle managers, for example), how those employees performed in certain courses, and what additional training they might need.

The LMS will easily track, for instance, the fact that Sandy Smith is a product engineer who has completed the entire learning track for engineers but, based on her assessment, needs a refresher course on a certain process because of regulatory changes. When it's time for Sandy to sit down with her manager for an annual review, the LMS can generate a report that lists every class she has taken, how she scored, and which follow-up training she took.

As we mentioned earlier, it may be easy for smaller companies to track this information manually, in a computer database or spreadsheet, or even in a three-ring binder. However, for multinational companies with tens of thousands of employees, an LMS has become a necessity. It's also valuable for companies that need to track training and generate reports for certification, ISO requirements, or regulatory requirements.

Here are some of the most common types of information an LMS tracks:

*Learners*

- Courses requirements per job classification
- Course registrations
- Time spent in courses
- Path taken through courses
- Number of attempts to complete performance tests
- Scores on performance tests
- Achievement of course objectives
- Achievement of learning milestones

*Courses*

- Available courses
- Enrollments, waiting lists
- Completion rates
- Billing data

Just as with other types of computerized systems, different users have access to different functionalities of the LMS. The LMS administrator, for example, has a login and password that give her permission to manage, add, update, or remove instructional modules arrange classroom and instructor schedules; set up learning events and collaboration activities; create student logins; and track student information. Figure 6.1 shows an example of what an LMS administrator would see when entering information into the administrator's module.

Like the LMS administrator, learners generally enter the LMS by typing in a login and password. Unlike an administrator, though, learners have access only to courses, class registrations, course content, and communication tools such as message boards,

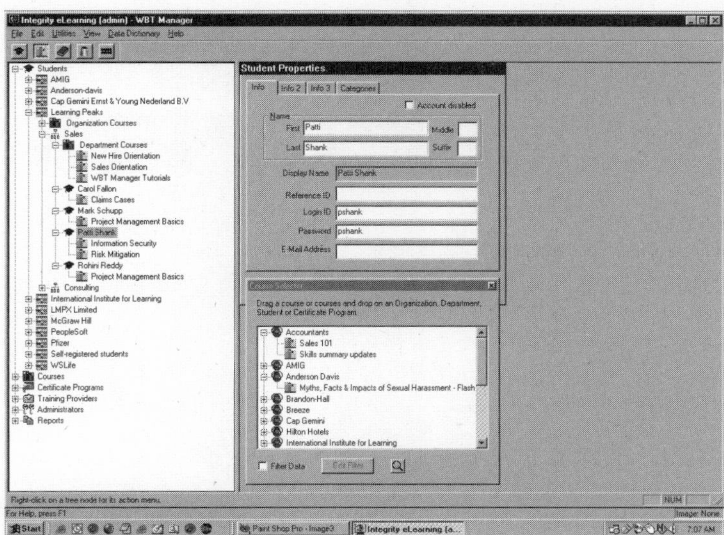


Figure 6.1. WBT Manager, Administrator View, Integrity eLearning
*Source*: http://www.ielearning.com.

collaboration, and e-mail. When learners log out, a record of which pages they visited and what courses they took goes to the LMS database for record keeping. Figure 6.2 shows an example of what a student would see when entering an LMS.

Some LMSs can do more complex things, too, such as integrate with enterprise resource planning (ERP) and customer relationship management (CRM) systems, but we won't cover those capabilities here.

An LMS can be either installed on your company's own network or hosted by the vendor. Think of it as the difference between a Yahoo e-mail account (which is hosted by Yahoo, so all your messages and data are stored on Yahoo's servers and made available to you via the Internet) and your work e-mail account (which is hosted by your workplace, so all your messages and data are stored

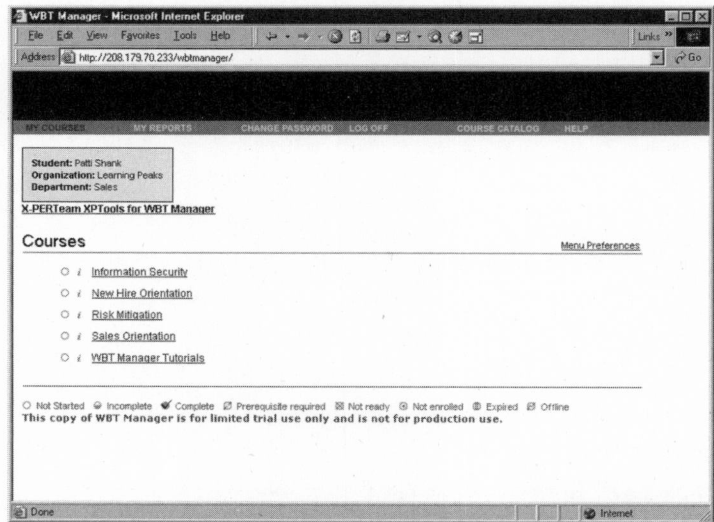


Figure 6.2. WBT Manager, Learner View, Integrity eLearning
*Source*: http://www.ielearning.com.

on your company's servers and you don't need to access the Internet to find them).

Installed and hosted LMSs will generally look and feel the same to the learners and administrators; the difference lies in where the data is stored and who controls the maintenance of the software. Each has its own pros and cons. A hosted LMS stores confidential information about your employees (test results, for example) on the vendor's servers, a prospect that makes some organizations uncomfortable. However, the vendor does the technical support and maintains the servers, which means your IT staff doesn't have to. Similarly, an installed LMS gives you control over the storage of your own data but also gives your IT staff the responsibility of fixing any problems that arise.

Which LMS you purchase and whether you go with a hosted or installed system are questions that deserve some serious time, thought, and consultation with your IT folks. The good news is that there are a ton of choices and there isn't one "right" system for everyone; the bad news is that the sheer number of choices can turn the process of choosing an LMS into a headache. If you're considering using this type of technology, see Table 6.1 (next page). It lists some questions you should consider before talking to LMS vendors.

One caveat about these questions: Some vendors will be so eager to get your business that they'll automatically answer, "Of course" to every question you ask, regardless of whether they actually have the capabilities you're requesting. The best way to make sure a vendor's "yes" actually *means* "yes" is to ask for references of clients who have been using the system for at least a year. It takes that long to learn all the quirks and flaws of any LMS and to figure out whether the vendor is as flexible during installation and implementation as they were during the sales pitch. When you interview references about an LMS you're considering, make sure you get the nitty-gritty from the administrative folks who manage the system, the developers and instructors who keep the courses going, and the technical people who support it.

Table 6.1. Questions to Ask LMS Vendors

| Question | Why You Need to Ask This Question | Answer |
|---|---|---|
| How many users do I need to support? | Some vendors can support only a limited number of users. | |
| Do I need to deliver content in languages other than English? | Some vendors offer foreign-language capabilities; others don't. | |
| Is the LMS compliant with standards such as SCORM, AICC, etc.?[a] | You want to be sure that the content you currently have can run on the LMS you're purchasing. The idea behind learning standards is that compliant content should be able to run on any compliant LMS. | |
| Does the LMS offer the types of reports I need? | If the reports aren't adequate, find out if you can customize your own reports without going through the vendor. | |
| Does the LMS deliver and track different types of assessments? | If you need to track specific questions for ISO compliance, for instance, make sure your LMS doesn't track only pass-fail assessments. | |
| Does the LMS allow for adequate levels of privacy? | In some European countries, you cannot report completion or assessment information at the individual level—only at the group level. Make sure your LMS offers the privacy protection you need in the countries in which you'll be working. | |
| Does the system seem easy to use? | Make sure the vendor shows you the set-up, development, and delivery processes so you can determine whether it's really as easy as it looks. | |

| Question | Why You Need to Ask This Question | Answer |
| --- | --- | --- |
| Does the system accommodate any unique needs I have? | You may have specific needs such as WYSIWYG capabilities, Section 508 compliance, multiple browser platforms, multiple operating systems such as Macintosh and Unix, etc. | |
| Does the vendor balk at showing me the things I ask to see in a demo? | It's a good idea to create a demo script—a list of tasks you want the vendor to show you. If the vendor balks at demonstrating a certain capability you've asked to see, this may be a red flag. | |
| Can I try it before I buy it? | Doing a trial run with a limited set of data can help give you a feel for problems and issues. | |
| Does the vendor allow me to customize the base product? | Some vendors allow you to customize their products to give you a look, feel, and functionality that's unique to your organization; others are less flexible. | |
| Does the vendor seem easy to work with? Does their philosophy fit with my company's philosophy? Are they likely to be around tomorrow? | You're going to be working closely with this vendor to implement the system; a "gut check" is one way to determine whether working with them will be a pleasant experience or a nightmare. | |

[a] See end of Chapter 6 for an explanation of standards.

## What Tools Can I Use to Keep Track of Online Content?

Chances are you probably have a lot of instructional materials in your organization: text files, PowerPoint presentations, graphics, pictures, animations, and video clips. The problem is that these materials may be located in many different places, and it's unlikely that anyone has gone to the time and effort of cataloging them and pinpointing where they're located. If you want to repurpose this content, you may spend days trying to find it—or you might waste time building content that already exists. For example, you may end up spending a lot of effort developing a detailed graphic to explain a complex process, only to realize your colleague in the Seattle office had already designed a similar graphic that you could have reused—if only you'd known!

A learning content management system (LCMS) is a type of software that brings all that content into a central location, catalogs it, and organizes it so you can find and deliver exactly what you need.

For example, if you were developing a new-employee orientation and needed a graphic showing the company's reporting structure, you could simply search the LCMS for the item. If the graphic already existed (maybe it was developed several months ago by the investor relations department for the company's annual report), you would simply insert it into your course. If the graphic didn't exist, you would create it and then store it in the LCMS so other people could reuse it later.

bottom line **Even though they are often confused with one another, LMSs and LCMSs have very different functions: LMSs track and manage learners, while LCMSs manage content.** Table 6.2 shows the primary functionalities of these two different technologies. (Systems vary, so this chart is based on typical functionality.)

These technologies are often used together to provide an overall infrastructure for online and classroom-based learning. LMSs man-

Table 6.2. LMS Versus LCMS

| Functionality | LMS | LCMS |
|---|---|---|
| Manage learners and learning events | ✔ | |
| Track learners and report results | ✔ | |
| Create, manage, and deploy learning objects | | ✔ |
| Create and administer testing | ✔ | ✔ |
| Create adaptive content (adapts to learners' needs) | | ✔ |
| Share data with ERP and CRM systems | ✔ | |

age learners and courses and provide reports about them. Therefore, they're most commonly used by learners, instructors, and administrators. LCMSs allow developers to create, store, manage, and deliver content from a central database. They're primarily used by instructional designers, developers, and project managers.

Not everyone needs an LCMS immediately, and some organizations don't need one at all. If you're considering using this type of technology, consider the questions in Table 6.3 (next page) before talking to LCMS vendors.

## What Are Learning Objects, and How Do They Relate to Tracking and Managing Online Content?

We talked earlier in this chapter about using an LCMS to find graphics or other pieces of content and insert them into a course you're building. Those pieces of content are sometimes referred to as *learning objects*.

You may also hear them referred to as content objects, chunks, learning blocks, modular content, reusable learning objects (RLO), and shareable content objects (SCO). You'll hear different terms being used interchangeably. To make matters worse, everyone seems to have a slightly different definition of what these terms mean. To keep things simple, we're going to use the term *learning object* here.

Table 6.3. Questions for LCMS Vendors

| Question | Why You Need to Ask This Question | Answer |
|---|---|---|
| How many people will be using the LCMS? | This could have an effect on licensing costs. | |
| Do I have remote content authors? | If you're working with contract developers who don't have access to your system, you need to make sure the LCMS accommodates remote authors. | |
| Do I need to create content in multiple languages? | Some vendors may offer limited language capabilities. | |
| Will I need to import content from other vendors? | Make sure the LCMS has adequate import capabilities. | |
| Does the content need to be compliant with a standard (SCORM, AICC, etc.) in order to be delivered through my LMS? | Be sure content is standards-compliant so it can run on compliant LMSs. | |
| Can I use my existing authoring tools? | Determine whether the authoring tools you are using can be used with the LCMS you are considering. | |
| Does it have check-in/check-out capabilities and version control/tracking for multiple users? | If you have many people authoring and editing courses, you will need a way to keep track of multiple authors and versions. | |
| Does it support multiple operating systems such as Macintosh, Windows, and Unix? | Some vendors don't support Macintosh or Unix operating systems, which can be disastrous to organizations that use operating systems other than Windows. | |

Learning objects are chunks of digital content that can be combined with other chunks to make instructional elements such as activities or lessons. Pieces of digital content (files in a digital format, such as text documents or scanned photos) are combined with each other to form learning objects, which are then combined with each other to form instructional elements such as activities or lessons. The following list shows how this works (adapted from Hodgins presentation, *The Future of Learning Objects*, NMC Online Conference on Learning Objects, 2003).

| *Digital Content Elements* | *Learning Objects* | *Instructional Elements* |
|---|---|---|
| text | overview | activities |
| graphic | concept | lessons |
| audio | procedure | assessments |
| video | principle | modules |
| animation | process | support or help |
| simulation | fact | courses |
| | summary | |

A database or LCMS catalogs the objects and then a learning management system (LMS) retrieves the objects and places them on the learner's screen.

In order to allow the software to search for specific learning objects, it should include metadata (information that describes characteristics of the learning object). Metadata describes the who, what, where, when, why, and how about any given data. For example, have you ever searched for an article in an online database? To find it, you typed what you knew about the article (characteristics such as title, keywords, and publication date) into a search field. Those characteristics are metadata.

The Learning Technology Standards Committee (LTSC) of the IEEE (Institute of Electrical and Electronics Engineers) has been working on learning technology standards (http://ltsc.ieee.org/wg12/), including one for learning object metadata. This standard provides a classification system for learning objects, much like libraries have classification systems for books. In this standard, learning object metadata include title, creator, keywords, version, language, typical learning time, difficulty, and technical requirements.

If you view the source code of a Web page (in many browsers: View>Source), you may already see metadata there. Metadata appears in the head section of an HTML page, in between the <head> and </head> tags. For instance, a professor who teaches in the technical communication program might include the following keyword metadata on her page so search engines can more easily find her articles and resource lists:

```
<meta name="keywords" content="technical writing,
technical communication, information design, information
architecture, web design">
```

Learning object metadata, like keyword metadata, also goes in the head section. Let's say you developed a small Flash animation about asthma symptoms. You might add the following learning object metadata that tells what the title is:

```
<meta name="dc.title" content= "Asthma Symptoms:
Beware and Be Safe ">
```

Likewise, other metadata might show the date that this animation was created:

```
<meta name="dc.date.created" content="2003–09–15">
```

**Delivering Customized Content to Learners**

So why all the buzz about learning objects and metadata? They offer the promise of delivering tailored content based on learners' needs, reusing the same content in a variety of places, updating objects in

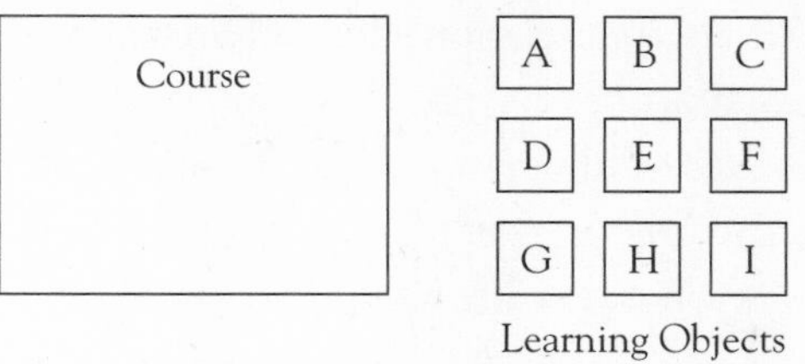


Figure 6.3. Course-Sized Chunk Versus Object-Sized Chunks

one place, and having updates appear anywhere the object is used. As Figure 6.3 shows, a typical course (at left) is created as a single monolithic chunk of information called a *course*. At right, the same course is divided into learning objects.

Here's a simple example to illustrate the promise of building learning-object-sized chunks instead of course-sized chunks. Let's say you sit through a weeklong course when you really only need the lecture from the afternoon of day two, the review video from day four, and the exam on the morning of day five. If the chunk size is *course*, a weeklong course is exactly what you get, whether you need it or not. But if the chunks are divided into smaller pieces—lecture, review video, exam, and so on—it's easier to deliver different pieces (learning objects) to each learner, depending on his or her needs.

Besides allowing users to access exactly the pieces of content they need, smaller chunks also make it easier to develop content that can reused and reconfigured. A video used in a sales course can be reused in a new-hire orientation. A graphic that depicts company lines of business can be reused in a sales course, an orientation, and client training. The glossary definitions developed for Module X can be used in Module Y as well.

Remember back in elementary school, when there was a map of the world in every classroom? When the map changed (like it did when the Soviet Union broke up), all the maps in the school needed to be changed, one by one. It was a time-consuming, expensive, royal pain. Similarly, if an organization's logo changes, developers need to go through each and every page of every course and manually swap out the old logo for the new one. Learning objects make it possible to change the logo in one place (using an LCMS) and have the change appear wherever the logo appears.

### Granularity

The jargon to describe object reusability is *granularity*. Granularity means the same thing for content as it does for pieces of stone—a grain of sand is more granular than a boulder, which is more granular than a mountain. The more granular a piece of content, the more reusable it is.

For example, let's say your boss just asked you to create a new course for call-center employees—and, by the way, it has to be done three weeks from now. You don't have to start from square one, because you've already developed a bunch of learning objects for previous courses that can be reused here. Development time is reduced because you can re-use the objects you already have and develop new ones to fill in the gaps.

In order to be reused and reconfigured, learning objects should

- *Have simplicity of purpose*. Learning objects should relate to a single learning objective or task.
- *Be self-contained*. Learning objects should not reference or depend on material in another learning object.
- *Be generic*. Learning objects should be applicable to many audiences and should not include audience-specific information or references.

This kind of content development is difficult to do. Even the experts disagree about how to do it and whether to do it at all. Still, the thought of providing exactly the content learners need and reusing that content has lots of appeal. Plus, creating good digital content can be expensive. If the content can be reused, the cost is more justifiable.

## What Are Learning Standards?

So far we have looked at how LMSs, LCMSs, and learning objects can work together to deliver online learning. Another term for this ability of content and systems to work with other content and systems is *interoperability*.

Interoperability is the focus of groups that are attempting to come up with learning standards. The concept of standards isn't new—in fact, it began in the industrial revolution with the standardization of simple items such as nuts and bolts. Manufacturers purchasing the nuts and bolts knew the standard sizes would fit their products.

Fast-forward to the information age, which has also been built on standards. The Internet exists only because of standards such as TCP/IP (Transmission Control Protocol/Internet Protocol, the fundamental rules for Internet communications), HTML, and XML. Because of standardization, the complexity that underlies these technologies is hidden from the casual user of the Internet. And these critical standards are what allow computers with different platforms and operating systems to use the same mega-network (the Internet).

### The Impact on Online Learning

Traditionally, the development of learning content has been somewhat of a "cottage industry." Individual instructors, developers in corporate training departments, university professors, or development groups in school districts have created learning for their students. The problem with this "craft" approach is that the instructional materials are mostly proprietary, making them difficult to share or reuse. Plus, it's expensive to develop instructional materials in this way.

Today, online learning is quickly morphing from a cottage industry into a global one. In fact, the largest purchaser and user of online learning in the United States is the Department of Defense (DoD). The DoD, as you might imagine, has an enormous amount of online learning content that operates on a variety of proprietary systems. Because of this, the DoD has been at the forefront of the effort to develop interoperability standards for online learning content and systems.

The DoD is working on SCORM (Shareable Content Object Reference Model), which is quickly becoming the leading model for interoperability in the online learning marketplace. The focus of SCORM is allowing learning objects to be deployed in any SCORM-compliant course. SCORM calls these learning objects SCOs (shareable content objects). The SCORM specification defines how SCOs are to be assembled and delivered by an LMS to the learner's computer. SCORM-compliant content should run on any SCORM-compliant LMS.

bottom line

**Interoperability means that a variety of content can work in a variety of online learning infrastructures. Interoperability saves time and money.**

You may have heard an alphabet soup of acronyms related to learning standards. Table 6.4 lists the most prominent organizations currently involved in developing online learning standards.

### The Impact on You

How does this affect you? For one thing, it affects your decision about which content and systems to buy. Vendors follow emerging standards and release upgrades to their products based on the new models. These upgrades sometimes have negative consequences for buyers. That's because content you developed in the past may not be compatible with an LMS designed to the new specifications. If your content doesn't run on your LMS, that means you'll spend a lot of time and energy revising the content to meet current standards. The fact that specifications are a moving target makes this process difficult for all. So what do you need

Table 6.4. Organizations Developing Online Learning Standards

| Group | Group Title and URL | What the Group Does |
|---|---|---|
| AICC | Airline Industry CBT Committee (www.aicc.org) | An international association that develops CBT and training technology guidelines for the airline industry |
| AIMS | IMS Global Learning Consortium (www.imsglobal.org) | A global consortium with members from educational, commercial, and government organizations |
| ADL | Advanced Distributed Learning Initiative (www.adlnet.org) | A U.S. Dept. of Defense initiative to achieve interoperability for computer and Internet-based learning courseware through the development of a common technical framework |
| ALIC | Advanced Learning Infrastructure Consortium (www.alic.gr.jp/eng/index.htm) | A Japanese consortium of academic, corporate, and individual members. Validates and documents specifications from other sources |
| ARIADNE | Alliance of Remote Instructional Authoring and Distribution Networks for Europe (www.ariadne-eu.org) | A European Union organization focusing on computer-based and telematics-supported learning tools and methods |
| IEEE | Institute of Electrical and Electronics Engineers (www.ieee.org) | U.S. body that develops technical standards and recommends best practices and guides for software components, tools, technologies, and design methods |
| ISO | International Standards Organization (www.iso.ch/iso/en/ISO/Online.frontpage) | Worldwide federation that promotes development of standardization and related activities in the world |

to know about specifications and standards as your organization develops learning content? The questions and answers in Table 6.5 should help you think through the primary issues.

Table 6.5. Specifications and Standards Questions

| | |
|---|---|
| Does my organization need to have a standards-based infrastructure? | This depends on the long-term content requirements of your organization. Creating standards-based content will allow you to develop content repositories, reuse content in different learning products, and share content objects with other organizations. |
| Does my organization need to create standards-based content? | Creating standards-based content is a major shift for most organizations, so it depends on your long-term needs. If you decide to do it, you'll need to install a learning infrastructure to author and store the content, and you'll have to develop a plan for migrating your existing content to a standards-based environment. |
| Why should my LCMS and LMS vendors be compliant to current specifications and standards? | Compliant LCMS and LMS vendors are able to work with any compliant content. |
| Which specifications and standards should my organization be attending to? | Organizations should support current SCORM (Shareable Content Object Reference Model) releases or have a clear roadmap for supporting SCORM in the future. |
| How actively should my LCMS and LMS vendors be pursuing compliance to emerging specifications and standards? | You don't want your vendors to be too far behind the adoption curve or too far ahead. Vendors should provide you with clear product development strategies and work with you to define a migration strategy as specifications and standards change. |

## Conclusion

As you can see, this is complex stuff. If you're feeling overwhelmed, join the ranks of millions of online learning designers, developers, administrators, and vendors. Since this stuff is less about instruction and more about the technology that manages instruction, it's not all that interesting to folks who primarily want to help people learn. Truth is, though, the background activities that allow the fun stuff to happen are important, too.

What you do with this information greatly depends on your role in the online learning process. If you're a subject matter expert who wants to develop instructional materials, it's good for you to know that your materials may need to work with some of these technologies. If you work in a small company, it's good to know what the future may bring as your organization expands. If you work in a large organization with lots of learners and courses, your company has probably already addressed many of these issues, so you'll now be "in the loop" when people talk about these concepts and technologies.

See the companion Web site for this book, http://www.learningpeaks.com/msoll/, for links to resources that will help you take the next steps to becoming more expert in this field.

# 7

# Evaluating Online Learning

If you are considering or have already started using online learning, you need to know whether the courses are valuable and how the skills being taught in the course actually transfer to the real world. Evaluation cannot be an afterthought, or it's likely that the information you get won't be very valuable. It's a complex subject, so we'll keep it simple, using the following questions as a starting point:

- What is evaluation?
- What aspects of online instruction should I evaluate?
- What's the difference between assessment and evaluation?
- How do I evaluate a course or program?
- How can I evaluate online learning?

## What Is Evaluation?

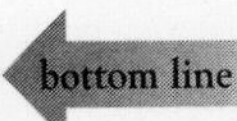


**At its most basic level, evaluation is about establishing what is valuable and then measuring it.** When it comes to online learning, you can be sure that learners will be measuring whether their effort and resources (their time, for instance) are worth it to them. And your organization will have similar questions about how well online learning works; the higher-ups will want to know whether the money they put into it has helped the company meet its goals.

## What Aspects of Online Instruction Should I Evaluate?

The answer to that question depends on what you consider important. A project manager should measure whether she got the project completed on time and within budget. An organization that cares whether this form of instruction is cheaper than classroom-based learning should measure the costs of each. Someone who cares whether online learning is more convenient for learners should ask current online learners for their views. Others will want to know whether this is an effective method for learning, and will measure whether learning objectives are met. Some folks will measure all of the above and more.

Like I said earlier, evaluation should not be an afterthought. Here are some critical questions to consider before the first person sits down to take your courses:

- What are the course or program goals?
- What will I measure to determine whether the program or course has been successful?
- What is important for learners to know and be able to do?
- How will I measure whether or not they know and can do these things?
- How will the process be evaluated?

## What's the Difference Between Assessment and Evaluation?

Measuring individual learning is commonly known as *assessment* or *testing*. Measuring course or program impact and effectiveness is commonly called *evaluation*. (Learner assessment or testing may be one of the methods you use to determine impact and effectiveness.)

When done well, assessment gives learners (as well as instructors, supervisors, and so on) valuable data that can help them determine whether they are on track with what's expected or required. It often takes one of the following forms:

- Formal assessment; for example, certification exam, final test
- Informal assessment; for example, prework self-assessment, checklists
- Performance measures; for example, checklist to see whether medical student performs all steps for informed consent, rating scale for copier troubleshooting
- Behavioral, cognitive, attitude, measures; for example, prehire tests to determine suitability for police work, aptitude for working with machinery

How do you determine what and how to assess? Those decisions start during the analysis phase (see Chapter 4), when you're setting instructional goals and learning objectives. When we design and develop instructional activities that allow learners to gain mastery, we should also build assessments to provide feedback and remediation.

There's a difference between assessments that help learners judge their own skills in order to get back on track and assessments that are used by others (managers, for example) to judge a person's competence, suitability, or mastery. Assessment for the purpose of feedback and remediation should be built into all instructional activities. But if you're judging competence or mastery, the assessment is usually saved for specific points in the instruction (such as the end of each module). Judging mastery is a higher-stakes type of assessment, so it's critical to use valid, reliable methods.

If you want to know what I think is important about assessment, take a look at Chapter 2.

**Instructional activities need to mirror the activities that people will be expected to do in the real world. And assessment should mirror how people are assessed in the real world.** How do we determine, say, whether copy-machine repair people can troubleshoot problems with the newest version of a copy machine? Simple: we put them in front of the copier (or a realistic simulation) and see whether they can fix it. In this case, a multiple-choice test might be fine for feedback and remediation while the person is learning, but it's not the best way to judge competence.

Another example: In the real world, customers may be the only ones who truly know whether the receptionist has good customer service skills. How do you assess the receptionist's customer service skills, then? Ask customers.

## How Do You Evaluate a Course or Program?

When you evaluate a course or program, you make value judgments about whether the course or program does what it needs to do. This type of evaluation takes the following forms:

- *Formative evaluation*. This type of evaluation is used during design and development to determine whether the instruction itself needs improvements or adjustments. It generally includes activities such as design reviews, individual and small group evaluation, expert evaluation, and field trials. If you're creating online materials, don't forget about usability testing (finding out whether users can find what they need and navigate the instruction without getting hopelessly frustrated).

- *Summative evaluation.* This type of evaluation is used after implementation. At this stage, you take a look at the "success indicators" (the actual results of your course or program) to see whether the instruction met the goals you set. You then make decisions about what to do about the gap between goals and results. It's important to figure out what your success indicators are up front, because measurement needs to be embedded in the process. Otherwise, you run the risk of haphazard or nonsensical evaluation. For instance, if you want to track course completion rates, it's much easier to embed this into your program via a learning management system or other software than it is to send out e-mails to learners after the course (which requires additional time and effort) and pray you get a decent response rate and truthful answers (unlikely).

**Formative evaluation isn't given enough emphasis in many online learning projects. That's a shame, and it often leads to wasted resources. When you spot problems early, they're much easier and cheaper to fix.** Problems found after the program is implemented involve greater expense and many other headaches.

bottom line

Summative evaluations are more common than formative evaluations, but they often stop short of obtaining real information. Part of this is due, I think, to a failure to determine what needs to be tracked up front and a lack of embedded tracking.

In the training world, the classic summative evaluation model is the Kirkpatrick Evaluation, developed by Donald Kirkpatrick

(1994). It purports to evaluate the course or program at the four levels shown in Table 7.1. (I say "purports" because the success of this model depends on how well the evaluation is done.)

Table 7.1. Kirkpatrick's Levels of Evaluation

| | | |
|---|---|---|
| 1 | Reaction | How do learners feel about the instruction? |
| 2 | Learning | Did learners achieve the learning objectives? |
| 3 | Transfer | Can learners apply the knowledge and skills to the job? |
| 4 | Results | What is the impact of improved knowledge and skills on the organization? |

*Source:* Kirkpatrick (1994).

### Level 1

Trainers and instructors often call Level 1 evaluations "smile sheets." Most know Level 1 evaluations aren't extraordinarily valuable, because they don't provide the type of information we truly need to make important resource decisions, as the other three levels do. Participant reactions, however, can have an impact on learning (Level 2). A positive reaction doesn't necessarily mean that people have learned (they may have enjoyed the course but learned little from it), but a negative reaction may indicate that learning has been impeded.

How do you design a decent Level 1 evaluation? Here are the basic steps:

1. *Determine what you want to evaluate*. This may seem obvious, but you'd be surprised at how many people copy someone else's evaluation forms without considering what they really want to know.
2. *Design a survey instrument* that will help you obtain the type of information you want. Ask for feedback on things you care about and would be willing to change.

3. *Provide some kind of incentive* for returning the evaluation. I recently took an online course in which we didn't receive our certificates until we completed the evaluation. Guess what—I completed my evaluation!
4. *Ask a few open-ended questions* such as, "What could be done to make this course better?" if you want feedback that falls outside of the specific questions you have asked. Open-ended questions are harder to analyze, but often yield critical data that cannot be obtained otherwise.
5. *Make questions as clear as possible*, and get feedback about the wording of the questions before using them. Sometimes a question that seems perfectly clear to you may be confusing to the person down the hall.
6. *Make surveys anonymous*, if possible—anonymity generally buys you more honest answers.
7. *Consider using online survey software* so you can easily aggregate answers and see trends.

### Level 2

Level 2 (learning) is the highest level of evaluation that many organizations perform, and most of them use skills assessments and tests during instruction to evaluate this level. One of the problems with Level 2 evaluations is that it's hard to know what to measure. First, many course designers come up with learning objectives that don't match what real people do in the real world. I once came across this learning objective in a customer-service class for receptionists: "Appreciate the difference between angry and frustrated people." Huh? Do we truly want receptionists to *appreciate* the difference? No, we want them to be able to discern the difference so they can help these two types of upset folks calm down. How do you measure "how well they can discern the difference"? Provide realistically complex scenarios that give learners the opportunity to make real distinctions and gain feedback.

How do you design a decent Level 2 evaluation?

1. In some situations, it's a good idea to use pre- and posttests to determine how much of the posttest results are due to the training. (As a recent doctoral student and now a Ph.D., I feel it's my duty to remind you that you'll want to get familiar with a statistics book to help you figure out how to statistically adjust scores so results are valid.)
2. Give plenty of consideration to the real knowledge and skills that learners will need when they use this content in the real world. Think beyond what is obvious or easy to measure.
3. Remember that just because the course is online, the evaluation doesn't need to be (and, in many cases, shouldn't be). If learners need to perform certain actions to prove they've learned the necessary skills, an in-person evaluation probably makes more sense than an online test. For instance, we might need to watch the copier technician troubleshoot in person, even though the troubleshooting course was online.

### Levels 3 and 4

Level 3 measures whether the instruction has transferred to real use. In other words, can learners do the job or use the content the way it needs to be used? Measuring at this level is difficult. It's hard to know what to measure and whether other factors are influencing performance in the real world. But it's an important level to measure because research shows that much instruction does not transfer to the environment where it needs to be used.

Level 4 measures results—outcomes such as decreased costs, faster cycle time, improved quality, and higher profits. From the business point of view, this is the reason for doing training. Level 4 is rarely measured, however, because it takes so many skills and resources to do so.

Evaluating Levels 3 and 4 is hard, of course. But I'd like to make the case that building in Level 3 evaluations—looking at whether instruction has any impact on how folks use the instruction outside of the classroom—is critical. Without this information, how do we know whether we're doing the right things? How do we prove our worth? How do we make resource allocation decisions?

### A Fifth Level?

Some are now describing a fifth level: return on expectations (ROE). The goal of ROE is to evaluate the cost of instructional programs against the expectations of those who contract for or initiate the instruction. For example, an ROE analysis of a management training program might include polling executives on specific goals for the program. Then, after learners emerge from the program and have time to use their knowledge and skills, those execs get polled again to see whether the program met their expectations. If it didn't, that means you need to examine the program and figure out how to improve it so that it *does* meet expectations.

## How Can You Evaluate Online Learning?

Evaluating online learning is the same as evaluating classroom-based learning, except we may be using technology to assist us in evaluation (or may not, as we noted with the example of the copier technician above). In either case, it usually isn't cheap. **It takes time and money to evaluate online learning—and even more time and money to do it well—but it's worth doing right. You don't want to make important decisions based on misinformation—or worse yet, no information.**

bottom line

Good instruction, whether it's classroom training or online learning, should do the following:

- Solve the problems that it was designed to solve.
- Help people learn certain knowledge and skills.
- Engage the learner.
- Do all of the above without overusing resources.

Of course, most folks don't have unlimited time and resources, so you have to select the things that are most critical for your organization. Table 7.2 lists some of the elements commonly evaluated and indicators used to measure them.

### Progress

What we're looking for here, in many cases, is a way to let learners know how well they're doing. Are they where they should be? Are there concepts they don't get? Do they need more help with certain aspects? This type of feedback should be readily available, and it shouldn't be scary. Learners should see it as something that will help them get where they need to be, not as a punishment.

Quite a few of the online courses I see have pretty pathetic feedback, if any. How valuable is a drag-and-drop exercise that lets me line up the potential types of disgruntled customers with the ease of fixing their problems? It might be fun as a limited indicator of conceptual knowledge, but it doesn't tell me whether I can apply that knowledge in real situations.

Instead of that type of exercise, consider providing extremely realistic scenarios (not the highly sanitized versions I often see) and meaningful feedback that allows folks to practice without fear. Even better, allow folks to role play and see how well they do. **Learners need opportunities to see not only whether they have a handle on the concepts, but also whether they'll be able to use these concepts in practice.**

bottom line

There are other types of progress that you can measure, too. You may need to know how learners are progressing along a specified skill or instructional path—for example, a certification track. In that case, you'd need to set up a tracking system that would notify stakeholders of completion or noncompletion of each step, and implement other events as needed. For example, if the copier technician didn't get a passing score on the "Replacing the XYZ Limiter" module, an e-mail might automatically go to the technician's supervisor, setting up a mentoring session before the technician retakes that

Table 7.2. Commonly Evaluated Elements

| Element | Indicators |
|---|---|
| Progress | Instructor, mentor, peer, or self-assessment<br>Progress along specified path<br>Progress with action planning |
| Mastery | Test scores<br>Performance scores<br>Job problems and performance trends<br>Stakeholders' ratings |
| Attitudes and opinions | Attitude scales<br>Satisfaction scales |
| Project completion and success | Resources used (e.g., time, budget)<br>Performance indicators (e.g., timeliness, field test results)<br>Project tracking tools (e.g., status reports, Gantt charts) |
| Course/ program success | Enrollment rates<br>Participation rates<br>Completion rates<br>Comparisons to benchmarks<br>Comparisons between classroom and online |
| Business results, return on investment (ROI) | Job turnover<br>Sales or revenue<br>Business objectives (e.g., compliance, regulatory)<br>Costs savings compared with classroom-based |

module. In other cases, the system might generate reports for managers at designated points so they can see at a glance how their employees are progressing.

## Mastery

You can measure mastery after the instruction, back in the real world, or both. (I vote for both.) Although online tests are convenient, it's not easy to design a valid, reliable test. If the test doesn't measure what you need it to measure, how valuable is it? And if folks' jobs depend on the test results, how fair is that?

Since the bottom line in most instructional situations is performance, why measure it so indirectly with tests? I contend that we should be measuring actual performance far more often than we do. Table 7.3 lists some activities you can use during instruction and back in the real world to judge performance.

### Attitudes and Opinions

We've already talked about Level 1 "smile sheets." Other types of attitude or opinion data might be valuable, too—for example, you might be concerned about the attitudes or opinions of other stakeholders. Do supervisors feel the training was worth their employees' time? Do they reinforce the learning when learners return to the job? If not, why not? How are execs feeling about the project? Do

Table 7.3. Activities Used to Judge Performance

| Potential Activities to Appraise Performance During Instruction | Potential Activities to Appraise Performance Back in the Real World |
|---|---|
| Observation | Observation |
| Hands-on task | Survey (customer, boss, peers, etc.) |
| Role play | Interview |
| Case study | Skill check |
| Simulation | Checklist |
| Demonstration | Demonstration |
| Model building | Self-evaluation |
| Self-evaluation | Peer evaluation |
| Portfolio | Work sample |
| Presentation | Work record |
| Concept map | Behaviorally anchored rating scale |
| Written assignment | |

they need more information? Any warning signs? Is anything happening inside the organization that might force changes to instructional plans?

These types of evaluations can be (and sometimes need to be) done as needed, formally or informally. Don't mistake formality for importance. Getting "off-the-cuff" information about how people feel can be extraordinarily valuable. Common "smile sheet" evaluations include surveys, interviews, and focus groups.

### Project Completion and Success

All projects have milestones and challenges. It's important to keep your eye on the project process, since the process can ultimately affect the quality of your instructional materials. Common project management tools include status reports and Gantt charts. These tools communicate to team members, stakeholders, and clients how the project is progressing against established deadlines and whether there are any problems developing.

### Course or Program Success

How do you evaluate the success of your course or program? Again, it depends on the goals you established up front. Because many folks don't take the time to determine their goals at the beginning of a project, they resort to using indicators such as enrollments or course completion rates. Sure, these indicators have their place, but what do they really tell you? It's hard to say.

Let's say you build a "Troubleshooting the Network" course to reduce the number of calls to the help desk over problems that average people could troubleshoot and fix themselves (like plugging the wire back into the wall when it pulls out). What do low completion rates tell you? Maybe they mean people are quitting the course without learning anything, or maybe they mean they're learning what they need to know and then logging out without officially completing the course. The completion rates don't necessarily tell you whether someone learned. What you really want (or should want) to know is whether the course

- Helped folks troubleshoot simple network problems
- Reduced the number of this kind of call to the help desk

Another evaluation method that has merit is comparing courses with established benchmarks. In a report called *Quality on the Line: Benchmarks for Success in Internet-Based Distance Education* (http://www.ihep.com/Pubs/PDF/Quality.pdf), the National Education Association and Blackboard (a provider of course technologies primarily for higher education) list benchmarks that indicate quality in online courses. Here are a few of the twenty-four benchmarks in the report:

- Courses require students to engage themselves in analysis, synthesis, and evaluation as part of their course and program requirements.
- Students are provided with supplemental course information that outlines course objectives, concepts, ideas, and learning outcomes for each course in a clearly written, straightforward statement.
- During the course or program, students have access to technical assistance, including detailed instructions regarding the electronic media used, practice sessions before the course begins, and convenient access to technical support staff.

These benchmarks are designed for higher-education online courses, but they'd work just as well for training or professional development courses.

ASTD has a benchmarking process for online courses called *The ASTD Institute E-learning Courseware Certification (ECC) Standards* (http://workflow.ecc-astdinstitute.org/index.cfm?sc=help&screen_name=cert_view%20). Here are a few of the standards they include for instructional design:

- Presence of instructional objectives
- Consistency of objectives with course content
- Facilitation of learning
- Practice with feedback

### Business Results

Remember back when you were just starting to think about building and implementing the course or program? At that point, you should have found out what business results were needed to make the course or program a success. You can measure business results quantitatively (more about that in a moment) or qualitatively. The important thing is to do it systematically: Figure out what you need to evaluate up front, build in the measurement if at all possible, make the measurements, and use the results to make further decisions.

The quantitative way of doing this is commonly referred to as return on investment (ROI) analysis. It's calculated with this formula: [(Total Benefits –Total Costs) divided by Total Costs] × 100. Sound simple? It isn't. ROI requires you to make some informed guesstimates of actual benefit and cost numbers, since measuring these things accurately is often too time-consuming or difficult.

For instance, you might want to measure the dollar value of people's time away from work for training. Doing this accurately would require knowing (and adding up) the salaries of everyone attending the training—a huge amount of information if you're training hundreds of people. So most people who do this analysis use an educated guess about the value of an average employee's time. Most execs understand that a lot of this analysis is guesswork, and therefore they don't take it all that seriously.

I personally feel that a qualitative approach yields more bang for the buck. Talk to people. See if they are using the training. Ask how it affects them. Ask their supervisors. (Do supervisors support the training? If not, that's a red flag.) Determine whether the goals for the training were met and, if not, what changes you need to make. **It's true that training costs money, but not training can cost even more. To be taken seriously, look at real business problems and how training can have an impact on these problems.**

bottom line

I recently worked with a client who was having severe problems with customers filing claims improperly. This resulted in numerous claims going unpaid. Turnover for telephone representatives was high, partially because it was difficult to withstand a torrent of abuse from angry customers. We first gathered data about why this was happening and identified a critical training need: Customers wanted to know how to file claims properly so they would be reimbursed. We determined that online training was a decent option and built performance support (simple job aids and mini tutorials) to help customers file different kinds of claims. Our next step will be to evaluate what percentage of claims get paid for people who use the support versus those who don't. Since one intervention doesn't always solve all performance problems, other interventions (forms that are easier to fill out, for example) are in the works, and each will include metrics for evaluation.

## Collect Your Thoughts

The worksheet on the next page helps you collect your thoughts about assessment and evaluation.

Course or program:

Goals:

- What are the course or program goals?

- What is important for learners to know and be able to do?

For these goals, what specific indicators will you use as evidence of success? How will you measure the following?

Progress

Mastery

Attitudes and opinions

Project completion and success

Course, program success

Business results

## Conclusion

Assessment and evaluation aren't separate issues from design and development. Before even beginning to design and develop, we have to figure out what has to happen in order for the training to be a success. The more specific we can be, the better, because these specifics provide us with measurement metrics that will help us prove value, evaluate the instruction, and make decisions about how to allocate resources.

See the companion Web site for this book, http://www.learningpeaks.com/msoll/, for links to resources that will help you take the next steps to becoming more expert in this field.

# Conclusion

By reading this book (or parts of it), you have taken a critical first step toward making good decisions about implementing online learning. Maybe you've decided it's not right for you or your learners right now, or maybe you're chomping at the bit to get started. Perhaps we've reconfirmed what you already know: This is mostly about learning and learners, wrapped up in a lot of terms and technologies that make it seem complex. Okay, so it *is* complex, but that's because it involves so many different fields: instructional design, programming, multimedia development, and information architecture, to name a few. It can be daunting to a newcomer, but after you start learning, you'll find it easier to keep learning more.

I wish we could sit down in person and have a conversation about what kind of online instructional materials you want to build, but in lieu of that conversation, I'll emphasize a few points from this book that are truly critical.

## Learning at a Distance Isn't New, and It Isn't Going Away

Distance learning has been around for a long time, and distance educators have used various media to communicate with learners. As long as people in various geographic locations continue to have a need to learn, there will be a need to teach and learn at a distance. The question isn't whether distance learning will happen, but how.

We use technologies because they extend our reach. If the essence of instruction is communication between instructor and learner, then any technology that facilitates communication is destined for instructional use. That includes printed documents, bound documents (books), mail, recordings (audio and video), phone, broadcast media, electronic media (computer disk and hard drive), and networks (intranets, extranets, and the Internet).

One thing is certain: Distance learning and technologies for learning are here to stay. That's not the same thing as saying technology is right for every learning situation. In fact, I spend a great deal of my time helping clients determine whether to use it at all. However, distance learning has successfully been part of our educational systems since the nineteenth century. Research clearly shows that well-designed and well-implemented learning environments, whether face-to-face or technology-based, are effective. Our task is to use them effectively.

## Using Technology for Learning Has Plusses and Minuses, and So Does the Classroom

Having an argument about which is better is like arguing about whether movies or theater performances are better. They have similar purposes (entertainment), but each has its own advantages and disadvantages.

The same goes for classroom and technology-based learning. We need to fully understand the attributes of each delivery method, when and how to use each one, and when to combine them. Classroom instruction is better, for instance, for immediacy and instant feedback. Asynchronous online learning gives people time and space to process what they're doing. Neither one is better than the other overall, but each one is better in certain circumstances and for certain purposes.

## Learners Must Have Need, Access, and Time

If learners don't perceive a need for online learning, don't have ready access to instruction, and don't have time to use it, it won't get used. I can't tell you how many times people forget to consider this. Don't think, "If I build it, they will come." Learning still takes time and effort, even if learners aren't in a classroom. Do they have the time? Is there an incentive to break away from their jobs to learn online? Are they free from interruptions? The answers to these simple questions can make or break your efforts.

## Good Instruction Means Real-World Experiences

Most of us have experienced at least one instructor-led class with a boring teacher, one-way communication, and no interaction. Chances are, it was dreadfully dull and not terribly conducive to real learning. If we know this, why do we put the same type of instruction online?

If we want to teach knowledge and skills in our online courses, learners need to do the kinds of activities that people in the real world do—and they need real-life feedback so they can improve. It's not enough to have learners read or think about the content; they have to *do* things.

Too much online learning is passive. The reason for that is that it's cheap and easy to develop page-turner online learning. My hunch is that a lot of designers and developers don't know how to build real-world activities into online learning, so they simply don't do it.

Giving learners a chance to practice their skills in a real-life context is not optional; it's essential. And remember, these skill-building activities don't have to be online. There's nothing wrong with teaching basic concepts online and asking students to practice those concepts in the field. The addition of social interaction is very powerful and sometimes absolutely necessary, depending on your learning objectives.

## Assessment Means More Than Just Tests

When I work with faculty, trainers, and designer/developers, one of their first questions is how to do online tests. I ask them to save that question until we figure out what we want learners to be able to do. Testing may make sense, but performance-based assessment often makes more sense.

Let's say you design a course to teach managers how to write performance appraisals for the people who report to them. Do you really care if the managers can answer multiple-choice test questions correctly, or do you need to see whether they can write well-worded and defensible performance appraisals? Real feedback is important, too. In the example above, chances are that peer review and feedback from an HR professional would be helpful.

I can hear some of you saying that the whole point of self-paced courses is that the learner is the only one who has to do anything. After all, HR professionals and the learner's peers already have enough on their plates. However, the bottom line is that it doesn't make sense to do online courses at all if they don't really teach what they're supposed to.

## Online Learning Isn't Always Cheaper

When online learning first came on the scene, people saw it as a way to save money over the cost of classroom-based instruction. Sure, it often saves travel dollars, but it can be expensive to develop, deploy, and maintain. And if it isn't designed well, it may not do what you want it to do, which is a big waste of resources.

On the other hand, the return on investment for online learning will be very high if it helps people gain access to instruction they wouldn't have had otherwise, updates people quickly on rapidly changing information, improves communication, or improves business results.

## Online Instructional Materials Benefit Greatly from Good Web Design

Online instructional materials should be attractive, simple to navigate, and logically organized, with clear and concise content. These notions are just as important for instructional sites as they are for marketing and informational sites.

## There Is No One Right Authoring Tool or Technology

If you're building effective online instruction, you'll probably need to use multiple tools and technologies, depending on content, learner needs, and the organization's resources. The average instructional developer uses more than five tools because no one tool allows you to design all types of instruction. That's not the same thing as saying you have to use more than five tools all by yourself. Many of us work in a team with folks who have different skills. Some folks provide content, while others build it.

Here's some advice: If you want to learn how to build instructional materials (and there are compelling reasons to do so), start by learning to use a general-purpose Web authoring tool like Dreamweaver. You'll be able to do a lot with it. You can bring in graphics, programming, and media from other tools and technologies, and there are very few limitations on what you can build. Proprietary instructional authoring tools may be easier to learn, but many of my clients find them quickly limiting, as do I. After you get Dreamweaver under your belt, you can start learning new tools as needed. Or you can find folks to help you.

## The Field Will Keep Changing Because Technology Will Keep Changing

This is a great field for folks who love to try new things, because it's always changing. It can also be frustrating, though, because there are always new things to learn. Sometimes it feels like running at 5 mph on a treadmill set to 6 mph.

No matter how much you know, there is always more to know. That's just a fact. And as technology changes, there will be even more to learn. Try not to be intimidated by this. Dig in, start somewhere, and keep learning. Find people to learn and work with. Exchange information and tips. Take some classes. Read books. Get on some of the listservs. Go to this book's Web site and check out the resources there. Play around. Help others.

This is a terrific field in which to be involved. We get to impact other people's lives, be creative, and keep our own brains alive and kicking by constantly learning new things. Sure, it can be frustrating, but it's worth it.

# References


Brennan, M. *U.S. corporate and government e-larning forecast, 2002–2007*. Framingham, MA: IDC, 2003.

Brennan, M., and Anderson, C. *The corporate e-learning market forecast and analysis, 2000–2005*. Framingham, MA: IDC, January 2001.

Dunlap, J. C. (2003). *The Problems of Practice (PoP) method: Connecting what we value as learners to our instructional practice*. Manuscript submitted for publication.

Kirkpatrick, D. L. (1994). *Evaluating training programs: The four levels*. San Francisco, CA: Berrett-Koehler.

Kiser, K. (2001, October). The road ahead: State of the industry 2001. *Online Learning Magazine*, 16–30.

Krug, S. (2000). *Don't make me think*. Indianapolis: Circle.com Library.

Moe, M., & Blodgett, H. (2000). *The knowledge web*. Merrill Lynch & Co. Global Securities Research and Economics Group. http://www.internettime.com/itimegroup/MOE1.PDF.

Moore, M., & Kearsley, G. (1996). *Distance education: A systems view*. Stamford, CT: Wadsworth Publishing.

Raskin, J. (2000). *The human interface*. Reading, MA: Addison-Wesley.

Rossett, A. (1987). *Training needs assessment*. Englewood Cliffs, NJ: Educational Technology Publications.

Sims, R. (1997). Interactive learning as an "emerging" technology: A reassessment of interactive and instructional design strategies. *Australian Journal of Educational Technology*. www.ascilite.org.au/ajet/ajet13/sims.html.

# Index

# About the Authors

*Patti Shank* is the managing partner of Learning Peaks, LLC, an internationally known instructional technology consulting group best known for helping organizations optimize online and distance education initiatives through analysis, planning, design, development, and evaluation. Clients include government entities, corporations, nonprofits, and higher education institutions.

Patti is well known for her independent, practical, and systems-oriented approaches to training, learning, and technology and is listed in *Who's Who in Instructional Technology*. She's a frequently requested speaker at training and instructional technology conferences, is quoted often in training publications, and has contributed numerous chapters to training and instructional technology books. Patti was an award-winning contributing editor for *Online Learning Magazine* and often writes for *Learning Circuits*, Macromedia's e-learning *Designer & Developer Center, Training Media Review,* and other publications. She teaches graduate instructional technology courses for the University of Colorado, Denver.

Patti completed her Ph.D. at the University of Colorado, Denver, and her research interests include interaction in online courses, tools and technologies for interaction, usability, instructional design, and instructional authoring. Her recent research on views of new online learners won an EDMEDIA 2002 best research paper award.

*Amy Sitze* has been an editor and journalist for more than a decade. For three years, she was editor of *Online Learning Magazine* (formerly *Inside Technology Training*). Before that, she spent five years as editor of a magazine for the electronic component industry. In her freelance writing, she's covered various business and lifestyle topics for magazines and newspapers. Amy is currently managing editor at *Gardening How-To* magazine in Minnetonka, Minnesota.

# Pfeiffer Publications Guide

This guide is designed to familiarize you with the various types of Pfeiffer publications. The formats section describes the various types of products that we publish; the methodologies section describes the many different ways that content might be provided within a product. We also provide a list of the topic areas in which we publish.

## FORMATS

In addition to its extensive book-publishing program, Pfeiffer offers content in an array of formats, from fieldbooks for the practitioner to complete, ready-to-use training packages that support group learning.

**FIELDBOOK** Designed to provide information and guidance to practitioners in the midst of action. Most fieldbooks are companions to another, sometimes earlier, work, from which its ideas are derived; the fieldbook makes practical what was theoretical in the original text. Fieldbooks can certainly be read from cover to cover. More likely, though, you'll find yourself bouncing around following a particular theme, or dipping in as the mood, and the situation, dictate.

**HANDBOOK** A contributed volume of work on a single topic, comprising an eclectic mix of ideas, case studies, and best practices sourced by practitioners and experts in the field.

An editor or team of editors usually is appointed to seek out contributors and to evaluate content for relevance to the topic. Think of a handbook not as a ready-to-eat meal, but as a cookbook of ingredients that enables you to create the most fitting experience for the occasion.

**RESOURCE** Materials designed to support group learning. They come in many forms: a complete, ready-to-use exercise (such as a game); a comprehensive resource on one topic (such as conflict management) containing a variety of methods and approaches; or a collection of like-minded activities (such as icebreakers) on multiple subjects and situations.

**TRAINING PACKAGE** An entire, ready-to-use learning program that focuses on a particular topic or skill. All packages comprise a guide for the facilitator/trainer and a workbook for the participants. Some packages are supported with additional media—such as video—or learning aids, instruments, or other devices to help participants understand concepts or practice and develop skills.

- *Facilitator/trainer's guide* Contains an introduction to the program, advice on how to organize and facilitate the learning event, and step-by-step instructor notes. The guide also contains copies of presentation materials—handouts, presentations, and overhead designs, for example—used in the program.
- *Participant's workbook* Contains exercises and reading materials that support the learning goal and serves as a valuable reference and support guide for participants in the weeks and months that follow the learning event. Typically, each participant will require his or her own workbook.

**ELECTRONIC** CD-ROMs and Web-based products transform static Pfeiffer content into dynamic, interactive experiences. Designed to take advantage of the searchability, automation, and ease-of-use that technology provides, our e-products bring convenience and immediate accessibility to your workspace.

## METHODOLOGIES

**CASE STUDY** A presentation, in narrative form, of an actual event that has occurred inside an organization. Case studies are not prescriptive, nor are they used to prove a point; they are designed to develop critical analysis and decision-making skills. A case study has a specific time frame, specifies a sequence of events, is narrative in structure, and contains a plot structure—an issue (what should be/have been done?). Use case studies when the goal is to enable participants to apply previously learned theories to the circumstances in the case, decide what is pertinent, identify the real issues, decide what should have been done, and develop a plan of action.

**ENERGIZER** A short activity that develops readiness for the next session or learning event. Energizers are most commonly used after a break or lunch to stimulate or refocus the group. Many involve some form of physical activity, so they are a useful way to counter post-lunch lethargy. Other uses include transitioning from one topic to another, where "mental" distancing is important.

**EXPERIENTIAL LEARNING ACTIVITY (ELA)** A facilitator-led intervention that moves participants through the learning cycle from experience to application (also known as a Structured Experience). ELAs are carefully thought-out designs in which there is a definite learning purpose and intended outcome. Each step—everything that participants do during the activity—facilitates the accomplishment of the stated goal. Each ELA includes complete instructions for facilitating the intervention and a clear statement of goals, suggested group size and timing, materials required, an explanation of the process, and, where appropriate, possible variations to the activity. (For more detail on Experiential Learning Activities, see the Introduction to the *Reference Guide to Handbooks and Annuals*, 1999 edition, Pfeiffer, San Francisco.)

**GAME** A group activity that has the purpose of fostering team spirit and togetherness in addition to the achievement of a pre-stated goal. Usually contrived—undertaking a desert expedition, for example—this type of learning method offers an engaging means for participants to demonstrate and practice business and interpersonal skills. Games are effective for team building and personal development mainly because the goal is subordinate to the process—the means through which participants reach decisions, collaborate, communicate, and generate trust and understanding. Games often engage teams in "friendly" competition.

**ICEBREAKER** A (usually) short activity designed to help participants overcome initial anxiety in a training session and/or to acquaint the participants with one another. An icebreaker can be a fun activity or can be tied to specific topics or training goals. While a useful tool in itself, the icebreaker comes into its own in situations where tension or resistance exists within a group.

**INSTRUMENT** A device used to assess, appraise, evaluate, describe, classify, and summarize various aspects of human behavior. The term used to describe an instrument depends primarily on its format and purpose. These terms include survey, questionnaire, inventory, diagnostic, survey, and poll. Some uses of instruments include providing instrumental feedback to group members, studying here-and-now processes or functioning within a group, manipulating group composition, and evaluating outcomes of training and other interventions.

Instruments are popular in the training and HR field because, in general, more growth can occur if an individual is provided with a method for focusing specifically on his or her own behavior. Instruments also are used to obtain information that will serve as a basis for change and to assist in workforce planning efforts.

Paper-and-pencil tests still dominate the instrument landscape with a typical package comprising a facilitator's guide, which offers advice on administering the instrument and interpreting the collected data, and an initial set of instruments. Additional instruments are available separately. Pfeiffer, though, is investing heavily in e-instruments. Electronic instrumentation provides effortless distribution and, for larger groups particularly, offers advantages over paper-and-pencil tests in the time it takes to analyze data and provide feedback.

**LECTURETTE** A short talk that provides an explanation of a principle, model, or process that is pertinent to the participants' current learning needs. A lecturette is intended to establish a common language bond between the trainer and the participants by providing a mutual frame of reference. Use a lecturette as an introduction to a group activity or event, as an interjection during an event, or as a handout.

**MODEL** A graphic depiction of a system or process and the relationship among its elements. Models provide a frame of reference and something more tangible, and more easily remembered, than a verbal explanation. They also give participants something to "go on," enabling them to track their own progress as they experience the dynamics, processes, and relationships being depicted in the model.

**ROLE PLAY** A technique in which people assume a role in a situation/ scenario: a customer service rep in an angry-customer exchange, for example. The way in which the role is approached is then discussed and feedback is offered. The role play is often repeated using a different approach and/or incorporating changes made based on feedback received. In other words, role playing is a spontaneous interaction involving realistic behavior under artificial (and safe) conditions.

**SIMULATION** A methodology for understanding the interrelationships among components of a system or process. Simulations differ from games in that they test or use a model that depicts or mirrors some aspect of reality in form, if not necessarily in content. Learning occurs by studying the effects of change on one or more factors of the model. Simulations are commonly used to test hypotheses about what happens in a system—often referred to as "what if?" analysis—or to examine best-case/worst-case scenarios.

**THEORY** A presentation of an idea from a conjectural perspective. Theories are useful because they encourage us to examine behavior and phenomena through a different lens.

## TOPICS

The twin goals of providing effective and practical solutions for workforce training and organization development and meeting the educational needs of training and human resource professionals shape Pfeiffer's publishing program. Core topics include the following:

Leadership & Management

Communication & Presentation

Coaching & Mentoring

Training & Development

E-Learning

Teams & Collaboration

OD & Strategic Planning

Human Resources

Consulting

# What will you find on pfeiffer.com?

- The best in workplace performance solutions for training and HR professionals
- Downloadable training tools, exercises, and content
- Web-exclusive offers
- Training tips, articles, and news
- Seamless on-line ordering
- Author guidelines, information on becoming a Pfeiffer Affiliate, and much more

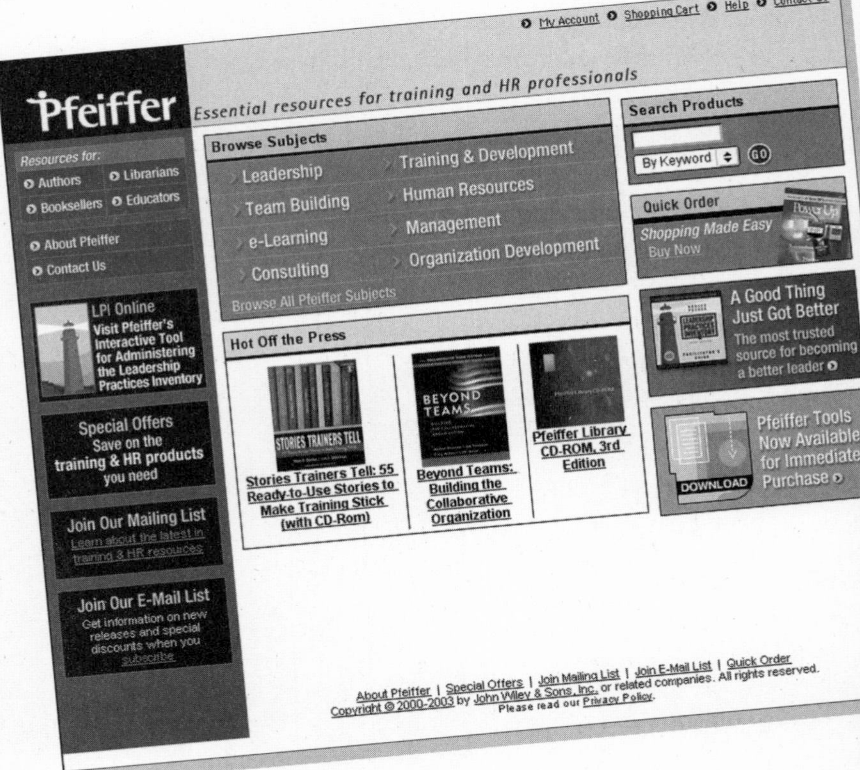


**Discover more at www.pfeiffer.com**